THE
REFORMATION

TIME
LIFE®
BOOKS

Other Publications:

THE GOOD COOK

THE SEAFARERS

THE ENCYCLOPEDIA OF COLLECTIBLES

THE GREAT CITIES

WORLD WAR II

HOME REPAIR AND IMPROVEMENT

THE WORLD'S WILD PLACES

THE TIME-LIFE LIBRARY OF BOATING

HUMAN BEHAVIOR

THE ART OF SEWING

THE OLD WEST

THE EMERGENCE OF MAN

THE AMERICAN WILDERNESS

THE TIME-LIFE ENCYCLOPEDIA OF GARDENING

LIFE LIBRARY OF PHOTOGRAPHY

THIS FABULOUS CENTURY

FOODS OF THE WORLD

TIME-LIFE LIBRARY OF AMERICA

TIME-LIFE LIBRARY OF ART

LIFE SCIENCE LIBRARY

THE LIFE HISTORY OF THE UNITED STATES

TIME READING PROGRAM

LIFE NATURE LIBRARY

LIFE WORLD LIBRARY

FAMILY LIBRARY:

   HOW THINGS WORK IN YOUR HOME

   THE TIME-LIFE BOOK OF THE FAMILY CAR

   THE TIME-LIFE FAMILY LEGAL GUIDE

   THE TIME-LIFE BOOK OF FAMILY FINANCE

GREAT AGES OF MAN

A History of the World's Cultures

THE
REFORMATION

by

EDITH SIMON

and

The Editors of TIME-LIFE BOOKS

TIME-LIFE BOOKS, ALEXANDRIA, VIRGINIA

Time-Life Books Inc.
is a wholly owned subsidiary of
TIME INCORPORATED

FOUNDER: Henry R. Luce 1898-1967

Editor-in-Chief: Henry Anatole Grunwald
Chairman of the Board: Andrew Heiskell
President: James R. Shepley
Editorial Director: Ralph Graves
Vice Chairman: Arthur Temple

TIME-LIFE BOOKS INC.
MANAGING EDITOR: Jerry Korn
Executive Editor: David Maness
Assistant Managing Editors: Dale M. Brown (planning),
George Constable, George G. Daniels (acting), Martin Mann,
John Paul Porter
Art Director: Tom Suzuki
Chief of Research: David L. Harrison
Director of Photography: Robert G. Mason
Senior Text Editor: Diana Hirsh
Assistant Art Director: Arnold C. Holeywell
Assistant Chief of Research: Carolyn L. Sackett
Assistant Director of Photography: Dolores A. Littles

CHAIRMAN: Joan D. Manley
President: John D. McSweeney
Executive Vice Presidents: Carl G. Jaeger,
John Steven Maxwell, David J. Walsh
Vice Presidents: Nicholas Benton (public relations),
Nicholas J. C. Ingleton (Asia), James L. Mercer
(Europe/South Pacific), Herbert Sorkin (production),
Paul R. Stewart (marketing), Peter G. Barnes, John L. Canova
Personnel Director: Beatrice T. Dobie
Consumer Affairs Director: Carol Flaumenhaft
Comptroller: George Artandi

GREAT AGES OF MAN
SERIES EDITOR: Russell Bourne
Editorial Staff for The Reformation:
Assistant Editor: Carlotta Kerwin
Text Editors: Anne Horan, Ogden Tanner, Harvey B. Loomis
Designer: Norman Snyder
Assistant Designer: Ladislav Svatos
Staff Writers: Lucille Schulberg, Gerald Simons,
John von Hartz, Edmund White
Chief Researcher: Nancy Shuker
Picture Research: Judy Gurovitz, John Hochmann
Text Research: Nancy C. Newman, Susan Apple, Alice Baker,
Carol Isenberg, Doris Kinney, Jeffrey Tarter

EDITORIAL PRODUCTION
Production Editor: Douglas B. Graham
Operations Manager: Gennaro C. Esposito,
Gordon E. Buck (assistant)
Assistant Production Editor: Feliciano Madrid
Quality Control: Robert L. Young (director), James J. Cox
(assistant), Daniel J. McSweeney, Michael G. Wight
(associates)
Art Coordinator: Anne B. Landry
Copy Staff: Susan B. Galloway (chief), Celia Beattie
Picture Department: Barbara S. Simon

THE AUTHOR: Edith Simon is a distinguished English writer who has published many popular historical novels, including *The Golden Hand, The Twelve Pictures* and *The Great Forgery*. She is also the author of the nonfiction books *The Making of Frederick the Great, The Piebald Standard* and *Luther Alive*. Born in Berlin, she currently lives in Scotland, where her husband is a don at Edinburgh University.

THE CONSULTING EDITOR: Leonard Krieger, University Professor of History at the University of Chicago, formerly was Professor of History at Columbia and Yale universities. He is the author of *The German Idea of Freedom* and *The Politics of Discretion*, and co-author of *History*, written in collaboration with John Higham and Felix Gilbert.

SPECIAL CONSULTANT FOR TEXT: Richard C. Marius, an assistant professor at the University of Tennessee, is a specialist in the history of the Renaissance and Reformation. He is a co-editor of the multivolume *Complete Works of Thomas More*.

THE COVER: *Hands of an Apostle*, a 1508 brush drawing by Albrecht Dürer, was a study for an altar painting in the Dominican church of Frankfurt.

CORRESPONDENTS: Elisabeth Kraemer (Bonn); Margot Hapgood, Dorothy Bacon, Lesley Coleman (London); Susan Jonas, Lucy T. Voulgaris (New York); Maria Vincenza Aloisi, Josephine du Brusle (Paris); Ann Natanson (Rome). Valuable assistance was also provided by Friso Endt (Amsterdam); Waltraut Eshenbach (Bonn); Jan Zegers (Brussels); Robert Kroon (Geneva); Barbara Moir, Katharine Sachs (London); Carolyn T. Chubet, Miriam Hsia, Christina Lieberman (New York); Erik Amfitheatrof, Mimi Murphy (Rome); Mary Johnson (Stockholm); Traudl Lessing (Vienna).

For information about any Time-Life book, please write:
Reader Information
Time-Life Books
541 North Fairbanks Court
Chicago, Illinois 60611

Contents

Introduction

It is well enough known that during the 16th Century a powerful religious vitality generated the movement that culminated in the founding of Protestantism. It is less well known that this occurred in a context of total social and economic change. Indeed, the age that is called the Reformation witnessed the shattering not just of the religious status quo but also of the secular aspects of society. The reorganization of medieval Europe that resulted produced the fabric of life as we know it today.

The 16th Century was the time when dynamic nationalism fragmented the vast empire that had held sway over all of Christendom since the Fifth Century and crystallized the modern nation-states. It was the time when the medieval guild system declined, to be replaced by economic individualism and, eventually, by capitalism. Perhaps most fundamental, it was the age in which men began to question tradition and to venture into innovation. It was within this framework of universal change that the religious Reformation took place, and the early leaders of the movement were reformers, not innovators. "One should help and cling to the Church," wrote Martin Luther at the outset, "for conditions will not be improved by separation."

The story of ecclesiastical reform as it developed into contending factions, and as it interacted with the political, social, economic and philosophical currents of the age, is unfolded in this book by Miss Edith Simon. Her book is timely because of the ecumenical movement of the 1960s. Thousands of Protestants now want to understand what caused the remarkable reform and strengthening of the Roman Catholic Church that began with the Council of Trent in 1545 and that led to the Second Vatican Council of 1962-1965. Similarly, many thousands of Roman Catholics want to resurvey the Reformation, that they may understand what it was that produced the churches of the "separated brethren" and prospered them.

In the past centuries it was almost impossible for anyone to read or write a book about the Reformation that was not biased. Many were written by Protestants who ultimately saw in the Reformation the foundation for all that is best in Christianity in the modern world. Many were written by Roman Catholics who ultimately judged the Reformation to have been the tragic cause of Church schism in the West and, therefore, the cause of the weakening of religion and the promotion of atheism in our time. If a historian were neither Protestant nor Roman Catholic his book tended to suffer from an anti-Christian or an antiecclesiastical bias. However, during the first half of the 20th Century, scholars, both Protestant and Catholic, began to transcend their personal religious orientation as did secular historians their secular orientation. But by and large there was no popular audience for such books.

Today the ecumenical movement is creating a market for a better historical treatment of the Reformation. In many respects our age is as awakened —and as much beset by turmoil—as was that of the 16th Century. And an understanding of that age can give us insight into our own. I believe that this book is a beginning in that direction.

EUGENE CARSON BLAKE
Former General Secretary of the World Council of Churches

NORWAY

*NORTH
SEA*

SCOTLAND

John Knox debates
with Mary
Queen of Scots,
1561-1563

IRELAND

*ATLANTIC
OCEAN*

ENGLAND

London

Henry VIII dissolves
the monasteries, 1536

Calvinists destroy Church
images in the Netherlands, 1566

Main

Spanish Armada sails
for England, 1588

Gutenberg perfects
his printing press
at Mainz, 1440

Paris

St. Bartholomew's Massacre,
Paris, 1572

Calvin preaches
at Geneva,
1541-1564

Geneva

FRANCE

*BAY OF
BISCAY*

Spanish Inquisition
begins, 1480

SPAIN

PORTUGAL

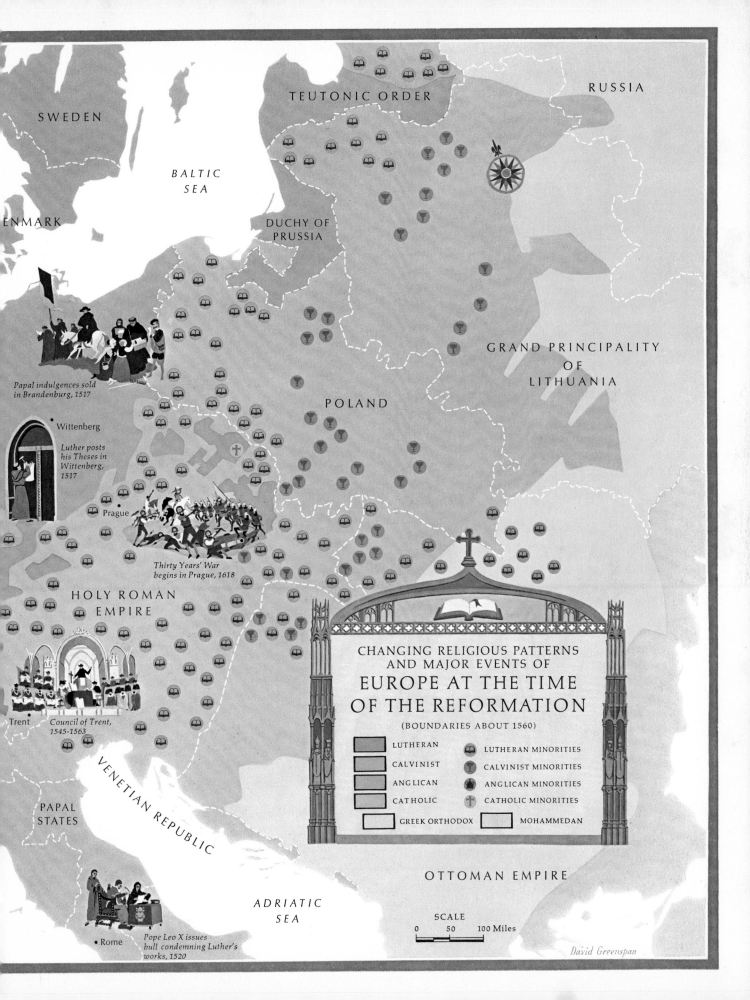

SWEDEN

BALTIC
SEA

DENMARK

TEUTONIC ORDER

RUSSIA

DUCHY OF
PRUSSIA

GRAND PRINCIPALITY
OF
LITHUANIA

POLAND

*Papal indulgences sold
in Brandenburg, 1517*

Wittenberg

*Luther posts
his Theses in
Wittenberg,
1517*

Prague

*Thirty Years' War
begins in Prague, 1618*

HOLY ROMAN
EMPIRE

Trent   *Council of Trent,
1545-1563*

VENETIAN REPUBLIC

PAPAL
STATES

ADRIATIC
SEA

Rome

*Pope Leo X issues
bull condemning Luther's
works, 1520*

CHANGING RELIGIOUS PATTERNS
AND MAJOR EVENTS OF
EUROPE AT THE TIME
OF THE REFORMATION
(BOUNDARIES ABOUT 1560)

LUTHERAN   LUTHERAN MINORITIES

CALVINIST   CALVINIST MINORITIES

ANGLICAN   ANGLICAN MINORITIES

CATHOLIC   CATHOLIC MINORITIES

GREEK ORTHODOX   MOHAMMEDAN

OTTOMAN EMPIRE

SCALE
0   50   100 Miles

David Greenspan

1

THE TROUBLED TIME

In the 15th Century northern Europe was a vast and doubtful place. The shape and size of the earth were uncertain; the Western Hemisphere was a blank, and the continents of Africa and Asia were practically uncharted except for the recurrent warning, "Here be dragons." The ruler of the world was God, Creator of a man-centered universe. Nature was dark and mysterious. There were few dependable scientific laws; the arbitrary miracles of divine omnipotence obtained instead. The divine scheme of life was the redemption of sinful man to the heavenly kingdom that Adam and Eve had lost, and the material world was a trial ground.

Since the zenith of the Middle Ages two centuries before, Europe had fallen on hard times. England and France had warred for 100 years. English nobles had connived and fought at home over the crown. Peasants in France, England and Germany had risen against their masters demanding more freedom and better living conditions. Worst of all, trading ships home from the East had brought in diseased rats that had visited on Europe the Black Death, a disastrous pestilence that decimated the population of the Continent all the way from the Mediterranean to the North Sea. Plagues recurred again and again. Trade sagged; fields went fallow; men who did not succumb to the plague died from hunger. Enrollment at the universities dropped, and many of the social and intellectual advances the Middle Ages had achieved fell into desuetude.

Peoples tied to the soil and subject to the caprices of nature have ever been superstitious, prone to propitiate an unfathomable deity with charms and to exorcise malicious demons with curses, and so it was in the dusk of the late Middle Ages. The people of this era shrank before the mighty example of the God who had consigned His own Son to the appalling death on the cross; before the inscrutable will that had caused to be carried off hundreds of thousands of dead in an inexplicable pestilence; before an angry God who showed Himself in the rustling of dry leaves, in the howling of distant beasts in the deep forest at night, in the flight of birds across the moon.

Fear was everywhere. Hellfire rather than paradise was the incentive to righteous living. Human

MARTIN LUTHER was painted in 1529 by Lucas Cranach, one of the Reformation's leading artists. Since Cranach was both a skilled realist and a good friend of Luther's, his portraits are probably the most accurate extant.

virtue was measured, and human training administered, by punishment. Ascetics flogged and fasted their way to heaven. Children were thrashed before they could reason. Servants and apprentices were whipped by their masters. Criminals were subjected to a whole catalogue of tortures. Murderers were boiled alive in oil cauldrons. Traitors were hanged by the neck, then drawn and quartered. Heretics were burned at the stake. Other offenders were strangled to the accompaniment of pious rejoicing.

Europe was still essentially agrarian, and rural life went on in tune with the cycle of the seasons. Grain was the staple food, and not until harvest time was there an abundance—and then only if fortune smiled and the yield was good. Even so, much of the produce had to be divided between storage to last until the next harvest, and seed to be sown for the next crop. Cattle and oxen, which in summer provided dairy products and labor, could not be kept alive on the scant supply of hay that remained in the winter, and people could not spare their own meager rations to feed the animals. Most of them therefore had to be slaughtered in the autumn for meat and hide; their flesh would be preserved by salting and smoking, and then rationed out during the long, lean winter ahead. The autumn slaughtering was a time of feasting and merrymaking before nature closed down and confined men to their cramped, shuttered dwellings, where they would mark the time until the new springtide, weaving cloth and making and mending their clothes and tools.

November 11 was the day of St. Martin, the patron of drinking and merriment, and his day was one for celebration not unlike the American Thanksgiving or a thousand other festivals that from primitive times have marked the passing of autumn into winter.

On St. Martin's Eve in 1483, a second son was born to Hans and Margaret Luther in the mining town of Eisleben in Saxony. In honor of the saint who watched over the event they named the boy Martin.

If saints and medieval demons were watching over the child, this son of a Saxon peasant was himself to watch over a new era—indeed, he was to help to bring it into being.

The dark and haunted world into which Martin Luther was born was in fact on the point of turning. A new spirit was emerging out of the gloom of the late Middle Ages. Life was growing easier, and some people were beginning to rebel against the old superstitions and fears. Once this process had begun, it was inevitable that Europeans would one day start to re-examine the whole fabric of their spiritual beliefs. When that time came, a leader would be needed to crystallize the new thinking. Martin Luther was to be that man.

In 1483, when Martin was born, Europe was just awakening from the late-medieval torpor. The towns were beginning to stir again with commerce, and the mines were thrumming with industry. The printing press had been invented and paper manufactured, and literacy was ceasing to be the province of scholars. German universities were proliferating.

Across the Alps, in Italy, the Renaissance had already turned men's minds from the promise of deferred paradise to the pleasures of life on earth; beyond the Rhine, France and England had ceased their hostilities. Farther away, in Portugal, a wandering Genoese, Christopher Columbus, was trying to enlist the support of a skeptical court for a plan to reach the wealth of Asia by a westerly route across the ocean. In 1453 Constantinople—for over a thousand years a Christian stronghold in the East —had fallen to the Turks; one effect of this seeming catastrophe was that a wave of fleeing Greek scholars flooded southern Europe, seeking refuge in the Christian West and bringing with them a

the critical spirit of late-medieval Scholasticism—or the pursuit of truth by painstaking logic—to create a different conception of the relation of faith and reason, revelation and knowledge. Scholastic theology had been built on the belief that a knowledge of God was accessible by reason, and 13th Century men had trusted in the power of man's mind to understand the ways of God. Fifteenth Century men were not so sure.

The invention of the printing press was disseminating not only Christian thought, but secular and pagan thought as well, and it was reaching a population that was growing increasingly literate. Some of the wealthy at first scorned printing as vulgar—which sometimes it was—and feared a drop in the artistic quality and economic value of their manuscripts. But scholars had no such fears, and many of them joined with printers to produce magnificent copies of ancient classics. By 1500 Europe possessed an estimated nine million books, compared with fewer than 100,000 hand-wrought manuscripts some 50 years before. No other invention has so thoroughly—or so rapidly—revolutionized intellectual life and society. The more men read, the more they felt the stirrings of independence, the more was traffic in ideas accelerated—and, with it, criticism of society and of the Church.

Nowhere was criticism sharper or independence fiercer than in Martin Luther's birthplace, Germany, whose growing wealth was in commerce and industry, and whose vigor was in the confident burgher class.

The German throne—or that of the Holy Roman Empire, of which the German territories were still a part—was occupied during most of the second half of the 15th Century by the Habsburg Emperor Frederick III. He was a weak and indolent ruler whose reign saw little accomplished but the marriage of his son, the future Maximilian I, to Mary of Burgundy, and the consequent acquisition

heritage of classical antiquity and a new intellectual outlook.

Europeans had encountered Greek learning during the 12th Century, but then it had come to them by translation from the Arabic. Now it was available in the original Greek, and scholars began to see the ancient writings in a new light. Before long they turned their attention to the font of Christianity—the New Testament—and when they did, they alighted on discrepancies between the original Greek texts and the Latin Vulgate of St. Jerome, which had been the accepted version of the Bible since the Sixth Century A.D.

The revival of ancient learning, literature and art had brought about a new attitude toward human beings and their place in the world. Formerly human accomplishments had been seen as a reflection of divine will. Now they were seen as worthy of attention in their own right. This attitude was known as humanism. Humanism combined with

of her holdings, which included the Netherlands, to the Habsburg lands.

The Holy Roman Empire was not a centralized state; it was a religious-political concept. It was Roman by heritage, Christian by faith and primarily German by language and location. In theory it was united in common interest, but in fact it was divided into more than 300 separate political units—secular and ecclesiastical principalities, and duchies, landgravates and free cities among them— and men were Saxons or Swabians or Nurembergers before they were Germans; they owed their allegiance to a prince or a city government rather than to the emperor. By Frederick's time the Holy Roman Emperor—a title dating back to the 10th Century—was only a figurehead; he had effective control of only a small part of his titular dominions, really only the estates of his family and their vassals. He had only a symbolic role and no real rule, because no German emperor had succeeded in cementing a centralized state as the French and English monarchies had done long since. Princes and towns restricted the Emperor's power; he could collect no taxes sufficient to his needs, and he could not maintain an army.

The real powers of the Empire were the seven Electors—princes and archbishops who ruled important territories and who, according to Germanic custom, elected the Emperor. They acknowledged the Crown in elaborate feudal homage but frustrated the exercise of imperial authority.

Hans Luther was a subject of the Elector of Saxony, which was one of the larger principalities of the Holy Roman Empire and the site of the rich iron- and copper-laden woodlands of central Germany. Hans was a free peasant and an opinionated, hot-tempered man who according to one legend had killed a man in a petty quarrel. Whatever the truth of the legend, he had left his father's farm because as an older son he had no inheritance. (The opposite of the rule of primogeniture obtained in the region where he lived; the youngest son, not the eldest, was heir to his father's property.) He moved to Eisleben, where he worked as a copper miner. He moved again to Mansfeld, began to save his wages, borrowed some capital and leased a small smelting furnace. After a time he employed others to work for him, and eventually he acquired half a dozen mining shafts and two foundries. Less than a decade after Martin's birth he was elected a municipal councilor in Mansfeld.

The career of Hans Luther, a peasant who might have expected to remain on the soil, testifies to the social flux that prevailed in 15th Century Europe. The bonds of feudalism, which formerly had kept every man in the station to which he was born, had loosed their hold. Aristocrats were impoverished, peasants were uprooted, and a new class of men were seeking their livelihood in trade and manufacture instead of on the land. In earlier days trade had been purely an exchange of commodities; lending for interest counted as usury, and usury was forbidden. Peddlers, having no feudal roots and selling wares they had not produced, were scorned as vagrants.

Now the scions of that lowly calling had metamorphosed into proud merchants; they handled goods for profit and put money out to breed; they created new enterprises, more goods and greater profits—which among other things could buy liber-

THE REFORMER'S PARENTS, *the dour Hans and Margaret Luther, often had heated arguments with their strong-willed son over his choice of career. On a visit to Wittenberg in 1527 they sat for these portraits by Cranach.*

ties, privileges and social position. A shrewd and self-assertive man like Hans Luther could rise from peasant to entrepreneur—and such a man almost always nurses even greater ambitions for his offspring than for himself. Hans Luther envisioned the profession of law for his son Martin.

The principles of Imperial Roman law, which had been revived in Italy in the 12th Century and applied to the French monarchy in the 13th, were now seeping into the German principalities. The development of a code of law was helping to create a class of professional administrators who were neither lords nor clergymen, but secular executives who became ever more indispensable, reputable and comfortable. If commerce was the route to riches, the law was the path to the courts of the great.

At his father's bidding, Martin Luther embarked on legal studies, but he discontinued them after a few months and retreated to a monastery. His father was bitterly disappointed and angry, but he remonstrated to no avail.

Martin Luther was a complicated man. On the one hand he was lively, cheerful, fond of song and companionship, and on the other hand stubborn, brooding, fearful of the wrath of God, given to tormenting introspection and self-inflicted punishment, all in pursuit of spiritual grace. If the social flux determined his place in the world, the medieval ethos of the God of wrathful judgment had a hold on his character. Entering a religious order must

have seemed to him the obvious way to acquire the peace of mind he so desperately sought.

Luther entered the Augustinian cloister at Erfurt in 1505, when he was not yet 22 years old. The chapter he joined was one of the most diligent of monastic groups. Monasteries had been founded with austere regimens designed to help their members to salvation, and medieval monks had done much to keep the culture of ancient Rome from disappearing under the barbarian onslaught, to train the youth of Christian Europe through long centuries otherwise dark and unenlightened, to fell forests and reclaim fields, to succor the poor and tend the sick. In Luther's time the monks were under attack for loose living and abuse of wealth and privileges. Some monasteries had lately been reformed, and it may be said that at Erfurt Luther experienced 16th Century monasticism at its most rigorous.

He undertook to fulfill his vocation with the diligence and zeal that marked everything he ever did. He practiced several forms of asceticism, fasting to excess and praying long hours into the night. He confessed his sins regularly and in detail, exhausting himself and confounding his confessors. "If ever a monk got to heaven by his monkery," he later said, "I would have made it. All my brothers in the monastery will testify that had I gone on with it I would have killed myself with vigils, prayers, reading and other works." Still he did not attain the inner peace for which he yearned.

If his superiors found his excesses exasperating, they were not blind to his intelligence; and eventually they sent him to study and lecture at the new University of Wittenberg.

Earlier in the 15th Century, Wittenberg had been only a shabby town. But one effect of the lack of unity among the German territories was the stimulation of competition. The Elector Frederick the Wise chose Wittenberg as the seat of his domains, which he wished to make the cultural center of Germany. He refurbished the town with public buildings, a castle and a new church. He amassed over the period of his lifetime a collection of more than 17,000 relics—among them some straw that was purported to be from Christ's manger, a vial of Mary's milk, and 204 fragments of the children slaughtered by Herod at the birth of Christ. He put them on display in the Castle Church, where simply for the viewing of them the faithful could gain indulgences—a medieval invention that meant a bestowal of grace intended to commute the punishment said by the Church to be due for the commission of sins. Indulgences were then, and would later be in a different way, the focus of much of Luther's thought.

Frederick's collection of relics was more than a source of pride and a promise of heavenly credit; it was a source of revenue for his church and for the principality. Pilgrims came from near and far to share in their blessings, and then as now, the tourist trade was lucrative.

Nevertheless, Frederick was not solely mercenary, nor solely simple and devout; he was ambitious for the cultural growth of his electorate, too, and to this end he founded the University of Wittenberg.

The university was only six years old when Luther arrived in the winter of 1508. It was small—it had no more than 300 students—but like many institutions that are new and small, it was agressive and open to novelty.

Luther taught moral philosophy and Christian theology at Wittenberg. By all signs he seemed marked for a brilliant university career; superiors and students alike thought well of him, and his mental powers ripened. But still he fretted about his soul, and still he could not come to terms with his God. His superiors were sympathetic and tried to help, but they were also worn down by his persistent anguish. His confessor told him: "God is not angry with you; it is you who are angry with God."

After two years of study and lecturing, Luther was sent to accompany a senior friar to Rome on a diplomatic mission for the Augustinian order. The Augustinians were required to travel by twos. Luther was young and inexperienced, but he had already shown himself a zealous and articulate spokesman. Probably this was the reason he was chosen, despite his lack of seniority, to accompany the man in charge of the mission. Many years later he was to say he would not have missed the trip, "for then I might have been afraid of being unjust to the Pope."

The two friars left Wittenberg about the middle of November 1510, around the time of Martin's 27th birthday. The roads were already dissolving in winter mud, and in the mornings they were encrusted with ice. Progress was slow and tedious. It might also be dangerous, for vagabonds menaced the roads and outlaws lurked in the great forests that covered so much of the countryside. Many impoverished knights had turned highwaymen, and so had unemployed soldiers, who chafed for adventure as well as livelihood. Princes and city leagues endeavored to keep order along the public roads, and some succeeded, but bandits and brigands still threatened in places.

Travel required more courage and stamina than money, at least for clergymen. The religious houses along the way opened their doors to fellow monks and provided them with free hospitality, and so did many a humble homestead. But if the traveler was overtaken by nightfall or storm, prayer was his only protection against wolves and bears and the demons that were known to infest the out-of-doors after dark.

The south German cities through which Martin and his companion passed were bustling with trade, banking and manufacturing, and Luther's thoughts

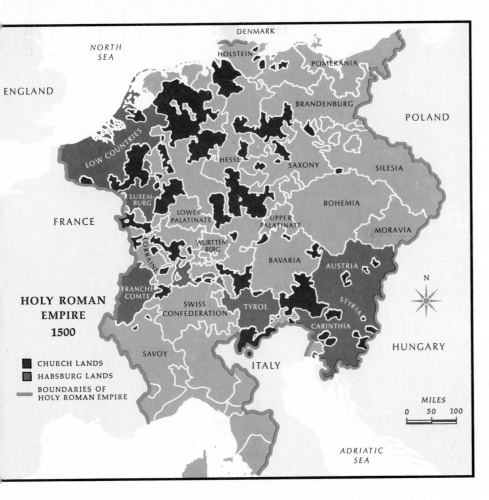

THE HOLY ROMAN EMPIRE, *established in 962 in an attempt to build a Christian unity in Europe, had by the beginning of the Reformation fallen into the political patterns shown here—an unholy muddle of more than 300 Church- and family-controlled units and free cities, often at odds with each other and obedient to the emperor when convenient.*

Map legend:

NORTH SEA
DENMARK
HOLSTEIN
POMERANIA
ENGLAND
BRANDENBURG
POLAND
LOW COUNTRIES
HESSE
SAXONY
SILESIA
LUXEMBURG
BOHEMIA
FRANCE
LOWER PALATINATE
UPPER PALATINATE
MORAVIA
LORRAINE
WÜRTTEMBERG
BAVARIA
AUSTRIA
N
FRANCHE COMTE
STYRIA
SWISS CONFEDERATION
TYROL
CARINTHIA
SAVOY
HUNGARY
ITALY
ADRIATIC SEA

HOLY ROMAN EMPIRE 1500

■ CHURCH LANDS
▪ HABSBURG LANDS
— BOUNDARIES OF HOLY ROMAN EMPIRE

MILES
0   50   100

on his journey as he recalled them later in life are an interesting revelation of the times, as they are of the man himself.

His observations were more practical than esthetic, but he was not blind to the sights. In Nuremberg he was fascinated by an invention that was appearing in towns all over Europe: a clock that struck the hours. In Ulm he was awed by the vastness of the cathedral—after the one in Cologne, it is the largest Gothic church in Germany, and except for its tower, which was added to in later years, it looks today much as it did when Luther saw it. In Switzerland he noted the ruggedness of the Alpine country. The Swiss people seemed to him hardy and sociable, but the shortage of arable land in the Alps caused him concern. It would not cross the mind of the 16th Century traveler, with his limited historical information and perspective, that the barren rocky cliffs he shook his head over secured the singular political independence that

the Swiss Confederation had achieved—an independence that was to be a most significant factor in the forthcoming religious upheaval.

Even with winter approaching, and with the passes and desolate tracks of mountain land to be negotiated, the traffic across the Alps was lively. For pilgrims, envoys, adventurers, artists and men of learning, all roads still led to Rome.

When he came in sight of the city Luther prostrated himself and uttered a half-prayer, "Hail Holy Rome!" Here was the capital of Christendom, the home of the Vicar of Christ, the sacred place that had known Saints Peter and Paul and uncounted martyrs of early Christianity. Luther had come some 800 miles on foot, and he was overcome with wonder.

Here, as in Germany and Switzerland, his observations were more practical than esthetic, but now they were mixed with the prayers of the awe-struck pilgrim. He took no notice of the treasures that would enthrall Goethe centuries later, but he was much struck by the size of the Italian figs and grapes; and when he saw olive trees bearing abundant fruit in the rocky ground he recalled the words of the 81st Psalm, "With honey out of the rock would I satisfy thee." The morals and the irreverence of the Italians caused him distress, but he was nevertheless able to like their kindness, their vivacity and—oddly enough—their tailors. Inherently charitable, he admired their hospitals, where patients were given white nightgowns and laundered sheets, and served their food on clean plates; and as a latent evangelist who would have much to say about the education of the young, he approved their foundling homes, where orphaned children were well fed, neatly uniformed and taught lessons.

The city as a whole in Luther's time was essentially medieval, with crooked and narrow streets, churches set in squares, walled fortifications and towers everywhere; but the ruins of the ancient past and the upsurging of the Renaissance were visible as well.

In the old quarter, the early Christian basilicas of San Giovanni in Laterano, Santa Croce and Santa Maria Maggiore stood among vineyards and fields. Cows grazed in the old Roman Forum, and goats gamboled on the Capitoline Hill. And everywhere there was rubble. Ruined Roman arches were interspersed with little medieval houses, some of them in open fields, others clustered together on crowded streets. Luther took no delectation in the ruins as did the humanists; he was insensitive to the grandeur of pagan antiquity.

Out of the rubble the Renaissance was rising. The new St. Peter's was under construction; the four great pillars were already standing in anticipation of the dome. Michelangelo was painting the ceiling of the Sistine Chapel, and Raphael was at work on the Stanza della Segnatura frescoes.

But Luther was not there to see Renaissance art; he was there on business for the monastery and as a pilgrim. There were monuments to saints and martyrs, dozens of churches and several shrines, for the visiting of which he might obtain a store of indulgences. When he was not engaged with the Roman Curia, he set out to see the sights, and like any modern tourist, he carried a guidebook with him. In his time making the pilgrim's rounds was an exhausting undertaking, as it was the fashion then to visit all the seven major churches of Rome in one day. The pilgrim fasted, that he might receive the Eucharist at the end of the circuit. The streets were largely in disrepair—many were not even paved—and it rained almost every day of the month that Luther was there.

Except for all the sacred shrines and churches, Christian Rome gave him misgivings, as it did many another pilgrim from the north. He was offended by the ostentatiousness of the cardinals' palaces and scandalized by the stories he heard of the popes, which were told by the Romans with irreverent amusement. Pope Alexander VI was said to have had bastard children; the current Pope, Julius II—called the *papa terribile* by his contemporaries—had more concern for the affairs of state than he did for those of the spirit. He manipulated treaties and men with abandon. He led his armies personally, astride a great war horse, hurling threats of excommunication at his enemies as he charged.

Julius II was the Renaissance Pope par excellence —one of a long line of frankly political, frankly Italian-oriented popes who disported themselves like secular princes. He patronized the arts, oversaw building construction and coined money. He is remembered to history as the sponsor of St. Peter's Basilica, the Michelangelo statue of Moses, and other works of art, but his chief concern was to regain for the Church the papal lands and power that had been lost before his pontificate. At this he

OLD ST. PETER'S BASILICA, *seen in a drawing by Marten van Heemskerck, had not yet been rebuilt when Luther visited Rome as a monk in 1510. Still a devout Catholic, he received Communion here but was disturbed by the casual cynicism of the Holy City.*

was successful. He inherited the Church properties in a state of dissolution; he subdued the factions that were fighting for them, and bequeathed to the pope who succeeded him a consolidated territory of considerable size. In January 1511, when Luther was there, Julius was away, laying siege to the fortress of Mirandola in northern Italy.

The native Romans were as profane as the Pope, and their blasé nonchalance was dismaying. They were unmoved by the sacred meaning of their holy city; they poked fun at the solemn piety of the northern Europeans; they joked about the rites of the Church.

If piety did not count for much in Rome, money counted for everything. Prostitutes, charlatans and beggars roamed the streets. Once when Luther was

saying Mass he was poked in the ribs by a hurrying Italian priest who muttered to him, *"Passa, passa—* Get on, get on." Southern languor and Latin manners did not prevent the Italian priest from saying seven Masses in the time it took Luther to say one; every Mass yielded a payment of money.

In all, Rome was part tourist attraction, part supranational enclave in the midst of Italy, and only part holy city. Luther was disappointed, but not yet disenchanted; he still believed in the authority of the Church, and the sins of Rome struck him fully only in retrospect, after the Reformation had exploded in Europe. Individuals might be corrupt, but he did not dream of imputing evil to the Church itself. For the moment he was satisfied. He had come as a pilgrim and had added to his store of grace, and the excursion gave some respite to his troubled soul. At the end of a month, their business done, he and his fellow friar turned north for Germany and the regimen of the monastery.

The monks at Wittenberg generally spent their few leisure hours in the garden beside the monastery. One day a few months after Luther's return his vicar general, John von Staupitz, called Luther to him where he sat under a pear tree in the garden and spoke to him about his future. "Herr Magister," he said, "you must become a doctor and a preacher; then you will have something to do." Luther countered with 15 reasons why he should not. He did not want the degree; it would mean a lifetime commitment to teaching and preaching, and Luther preferred—or so he seems to have thought at the time—to seek his salvation through the isolated prayer and meditation of monastic life. Staupitz reproached him for his reluctance, but Luther replied, "Herr Staupitz, you will bring me to my death. I will never endure it for three months."

"Don't you know that Our Lord God has many great matters to attend to?" Staupitz asked. "For these He needs clever people to advise Him. If you should die, you will be received into His council in heaven, for He, too, has need of some doctors."

The vicar general jested, but he clearly was in earnest. Luther therefore entered the University of Wittenberg once more, this time to prepare for the doctorate and to lecture on the Bible.

He still had no thought of causing the upheaval that would shake the Church and the Christian world; but even from the beginning his teaching was out of the ordinary. One of the older professors at the University exclaimed: "This monk will confuse all the doctors. He will start a new religion and reform the whole Roman Church, for he bases his theology on the writings of the Prophets and the Apostles. He stands on the words of Christ, which no philosophy or sophistry can upset or op-

pose, be it that of the Scotists, the Albertists [or] the Thomists."

A year later, in the Elector Frederick's Castle Church in Wittenberg, the degree was conferred upon him. He was licensed to "defend the evangelical truth according to his strength." He swore obedience to the dean and masters of the theological faculty and took an oath "not to teach vain and foreign doctrines which are condemned by the Church and hurt pious ears." The presiding professor, Bodenstein von Carlstadt, placed a woolen beret on Luther's head and a silver doctor's ring on his finger. Luther then engaged in the customary disputation. When it was over his fellow students carried him on their shoulders through the streets of Wittenberg, and the church bells tolled in celebration with them.

The year was 1512. A great deal had happened in the 29 years since Luther's birth. Columbus had found support for his scheme in Spain and had discovered the New World, and all nations were now vying with one another in foreign trade and conquest. The material world was becoming more and more definite and spiritual ideals more confused, as the printing press spread information and humanist studies inspired ideas of doctrinal difference. The contemporary era was coming to seem in peril, and early Christianity seemed in the distance a paradise of simplicity and truth from which modern man had strayed. The nations were becoming ever more conscious of their nationalities, and the faithful were smarting over the shortcomings of society and of the Church.

Something of Luther's uneasiness was everywhere. As he began at Wittenberg to prepare his lectures on the Bible in a quiet tower study—a sanctuary where he would find his calling and work for the rest of his life—the world was priming for an explosion. The ideas he was to formulate, conceived in the most fervent piety, would touch it off.

LUSTY VILLAGERS *of a Flemish town while away a free afternoon outside a tavern, drinking, squabbling and courting to the squalling of a bagpipe.*

THE PEASANT'S LIFE

At the opening of the 16th Century, some four out of five Europeans were still working the soil. Many had risen from abject serfdom to become free or tenant farmers, paid laborers or village artisans. But most peasants were still heavily burdened with taxes and services to their lords, the owners of their land. In many places a peasant could not even die without paying a tax to his master—in some cases as much as half his estate. Only within his own community could he find a measure of companionship and relief. Isolated, self-sufficient and close-knit, the peasant village was united by its communal pleasures as well as by shared hardship. Its joys and sorrows were recorded by many artists, most notably *(above)* by the Flemish master Pieter Brueghel. Some of their scenes suggest the peasant's rough sense of fun, others his resentment and despair—emotions that gave rise at first to protests and petitions, and finally to bloody revolt.

Laboring for Church, Lord and Family

Living in the shadow of a manor house or castle, many a peasant of the Reformation labored not only to sustain himself and his dependents but also to meet the demands of his lord. It was a hard life. The peasant's cottage—built of timber, clay and rubble with a roof of thatch and a floor of earth—was dim, dirty and, in winter, bitterly cold. Back of the cottage was a small garden plot, and sometimes a chicken coop, pigsty or cowshed; backyard produce was needed to supplement the often meager harvest.

Before he could feed his own family, the peasant paid two masters. To the Church went a "great tithe," or tenth, of his grain, another tithe of fruit and vegetables, a third tithe of livestock. To his lord, he twice a year yielded up a fixed percentage of all he produced as rent for his land. Even more irksome was the time exacted for personal service on the lord's domain—in some parts of Germany, 60 days. These days, often falling when the peasant most needed the time for his own crops, were spent doing anything the master ordained—including beating the bushes for the noble pastime of the hunt. "We have to run after the game all day without food or drink," one peasant protest declared, "and we get our pay in curses and kicks."

A BUSTLING KITCHEN, *more prosperous than most, brims with food for a harvest holiday in this painting by Pieter Aertsen. In winter, the whole family often slept around the fire in this one room.*

A COASTAL VILLAGE *weathers a winter storm in Brueghel's "Dark Day" (left). Aloof from this cluster of crude buildings—including a tavern (foreground) and a church—rises the lord's castle.*

SPRING PLANTING *of a lord's formal gardens, painted by Abel Grimer, is done by stooping peasants.*

A SUMMER HARVEST *is reaped and slowly carried, a basket at a time, from outlying fields to the village.*

THE FALL DRIVE *(by Brueghel) brings cattle from pasture to winter quarters or the slaughterhouse.*

An Annual Cycle of Rural Tasks

A peasant's daily work was rigidly dictated by the cycle of seasons and often by an agricultural system handed down from medieval times. Arable land around many villages was still divided into three great fields in which an individual worker had the use of scattered plots. In one he grew wheat or rye for bread; in a second, barley for beer and oats for cattle; the third was left fallow for future crops. The peasant's implements were crude and few: a small wooden plow, sometimes pulled by a horse or an ox; a scythe for reaping; a flail for threshing grain.

After the harvest was in, the herds were rounded up from the common pasture or brought down from the hills. Some of the lord's cattle went into his barns, but for lack of shelter and fodder peasants slaughtered most of their own livestock in the fall; few could survive the winter outdoors.

Oftentimes, the only way a hungry man could bring his family through the lean months was by poaching—killing for food the quail, pheasant, doves and deer which the lord kept for his own hunting pleasure (and which often nibbled away at the crops). The penalty for poaching could be severe. In the words of one peasant complaint, "those animals which do us harm, we are forbidden to hurt . . . and to disobey is to have one's eyes put out."

FOOD FOR WINTER *is hurried in through a snowstorm in this village scene by Lucas van Valkenborch.*

A BRIDAL SUPPER *is topped off by flatcakes brought in on a door. The plump bride sits demurely at left while the priest talks with a guest at right.*

The Boisterous Pageant of a Peasant Wedding

HAPPY CELEBRANTS *make the most of the occasion. Having emptied their bowls and drained their mugs, these three wedding guests are ready for more.*

Although a serf often could not even marry without getting his lord's permission (and paying him an extra tax), prosperous peasants celebrated the event with lavish generosity; sometimes a family spent as much on a wedding feast as it would to buy a small house. On such occasions, manners were coarse, talk free and drinking prodigious. Undernourished and overworked, a peasant consumed as much as a gallon of wine or beer on an average day; at weddings, he outdid himself. The Brueghel paintings and details here show some of the high spirit and crude humor with which countryfolk, released from their toil, shared a rare moment of joy.

A WEDDING DANCE *brings all the villagers together, twisting and reeling to the piper's tune. Even on such dress occasions, men wore their knives.*

Rough Fun on Holy Days

Farm and Church holidays were free days in the peasant's calendar of labor, and he greeted them with a robust irreverence that often alarmed the higher clergy. These gentlemen of the Church deplored the sinful transgressions that accompanied rural merrymaking, yet they continued to create even

more occasions for it: by the start of the 16th Century, a score of saints' days were observed each year. The glee which countryfolk brought to their holidays is suggested in this carnival scene by Adriaen van de Venne. As a few genteel townsfolk look on, entertainers parade in a fantastic array of household utensils. In front, a grizzled patriarch holds up a cape on a broom and wears a giant fishhook. Behind him waltzes a "knight" in beer-barrel armor and his "bride" in a tub hat and a necklace of eggshells. A shoulder-borne flutist and two hunchbacks provide a din of music for the frolicking ranks behind.

Victims of Terror
in an Age of Violence

The 16th Century was a time of fierce passions and constant strife. "None goeth unarmed in public," one contemporary chronicler wrote; "each hath his sword by his side for any chance emergency." The emergencies were not hard to find. Between periodic wars, mercenary troops, their wages cut off, moved around the countryside attacking merchant trains and occasionally plundering peasant villages. In 1529, one band of freebooters boasted of having burned 52 churches in England as well as stealing tremendous stores of private property. Already oppressed by their own cruel lords, peasants often fought back savagely against the brigands *(below)*.

MURDER AT AN INN *is short, grim work for a pair of peasants, who are knifing a soldier in this painting by Marten van Clève. A second soldier lies dead beside an overturned table while a third rides in through the door to join the bloody fray.*

THE MASSACRE OF THE INNOCENTS, *a Biblical theme, becomes contemporary reality in Brueghel's picture of a village being sacked by soldiers. Remote towns provided easy targets for roaming brigands, and inhabitants had to plead for their lives.*

Casualties of Cruel Times

The disintegration of the feudal system provided increased opportunities for some peasants, but for others it meant only the freedom to starve under still harsher taxes and rents. Mounting resentments finally burst out in Germany in the

bloody Peasants' War of 1524. The result was only greater disaster: some 100,000 rebels were killed and 50,000 left homeless, their villages and fields destroyed. Famine and disease erupted afresh; beggars filled the cities and bandits prowled the roads. The most pitiable victims were the orphaned, the aged, the crippled and the sick. Cut off from former charities, their plight is suggested by Brueghel's parable of the blind vagabonds *(below)*, following their hapless leader into a ditch.

2

THE REFORMER

The Church in Luther's time had no determinate territory, but it was a state. It had its monarch in the pope, its princes in the prelates, its subjects in all of Western Christendom. It had legislative assemblies in ecumenical councils, a constitution in canon law, judicial courts and a fiscal agency in the Curia. It went to war, it negotiated treaties, it collected taxes.

This comprehensive authority of the Church was based on long tradition and an overlay of written law, but it did not go unchallenged. Kings opposed the hand of the Church in their domestic power and in their revenues. Scholars questioned interpretations of dogma. Men of all classes chafed under the tithes, the taxes levied on the laity.

The grievances against the Church were many, but none was more bitter than the grievance over its wealth. The Church took annual tribute from kings. It required fees of bishops on their appointment. It levied separate taxes for the building of churches, the fighting of wars and countless other undertakings.

A lucrative source of Church income, and one that was to become a cause célèbre, was the indulgence. Indulgences remitted the punishment due for sins, and in exchange the penitent made a cash contribution to the Church.

The forgiveness of God was contingent upon confession, penitence and satisfaction, or penance. During the Middle Ages penances had been severe indeed; they had consisted of such acts as seven years' fasting on bread and water, or long and arduous pilgrimages. Over the centuries the indulgence had developed as a substitute: the payment of money replaced the performance of the deed of penance. The idea was not so baldly mercenary as it appears at first glance; it arose out of the Germanic legal idea that corporal punishment for crimes was convertible to payments of money—in other words, to fines. As money and indulgences became intertwined, however, the idea became subject to abuse. Simple folk came to suppose that the payment of money would justify them in the eyes of God, as so often it did in the eyes of men.

Originally each indulgence was issued for a special case; by Luther's time indulgences were issued generally. The faithful would attend special services, or visit sacred shrines, or venerate relics, as did Luther himself on his journey to Rome; they would make offerings of money for the privilege, and receive in return certificates of the indulgences they had acquired. Official Church doctrine did not specifically say so, but the masses believed they were taking out insurance on salvation.

The Church was not blind to its shortcomings; it clearly saw the gap between its ideals and its practice, and it often reviewed questions of papal power, institutional corruption and even of doctrine. But though it acknowledged the need for correction, it adamantly asserted the right to correct itself from within and recognized no authority outside of Rome to do the work.

Proponents of reform fell generally into three categories. There were spiritual reformers, who deplored worldly pursuits and advocated programs of piety and austerity. There were advocates of the conciliar theory, who wished to see an ecumenical council reform the Church institutionally. Finally, there were the humanists, who believed that knowledge of the Bible would restore the purity that had characterized the early Church.

The first of these groups, the spiritual reformers, were preachers who addressed themselves to the people. They believed that society was corrupt, that state measures would be of no avail, and that a return to piety was the only route to human salvation. The spiritual reformers won considerable popular acceptance, but received mixed recognition from the Church itself. Some, whose teachings were orthodox, were tolerated by Rome; but others who caused unrest and disobedience among the masses were condemned as heretics.

The conciliarists were primarily statesmen, secular and ecclesiastical, who addressed themselves to Rome. Some were kings and royal ministers for whom reform meant liberation from Roman interference in their national politics, freedom to ap-

point politically favorable bishops, and release from the drain of gold and silver to Rome. Some were men who were simply jealous of national identity and objected to the all-Italian composition of the Curia. Others were theologians who believed that a council, as a parliamentary body of the Church, would provide a check on the vagaries of an unscrupulous pope.

The conciliar movement in the Church had, of course, a parallel in the parliamentary movement in the secular governments. Yet it made much less headway than political parliamentarianism. The main reason was that Church councils, which had been convened periodically in the past, had proved to be ineffectual and subject to political pressure. The bishops and cardinals who sat on them often served in secular government as ministers to kings. They therefore had conflicting loyalties—and monarchs did not hesitate to take advantage of this fact and use the councils for their own ends. For this reason, the popes, understandably, discouraged the growth of the conciliar movement.

The humanists, the third group of reformers, differed from the conciliarists (though there were conciliarists among them) in having interests more cosmopolitan than national, and from the preachers of piety (though their concern was with morality) in laying emphasis on the intellect rather than on divine inspiration.

Above all else, the humanists deplored ignorance, and they exalted the power of the educated human mind. They interpreted dogma figuratively rather than literally, and thought wrangles over such matters as sacraments and grace were foolish and disruptive. They believed that man was essentially good, and they looked to education for his improvement. If men were educated, they believed, their standard of ethics would naturally rise—to the benefit of society and Church alike.

The humanist movement originated in Renais-

"Truly the yoke of Christ would be sweet, and His burdens light, if petty human institutions added nothing to what He Himself imposed. He commanded us nothing save love for one another."

Surrounded by books and flowers which suggest his erudition and love of beauty, Erasmus of Rotterdam is shown at the little writing desk where he framed such thoughts as those expressed in the quotation above, which values the teachings of Christ above the intercession of the Church. Behind the robed philosopher appear the elaborate title, date and signature of Albrecht Dürer, who made the engraving. Dürer paid homage to Erasmus with the inscription in Greek at the center: "His writings depict him even better."

sance Italy, and men drawn there by its luster carried it north. One such scholar was Lefèvre of Etaples, a theologian and classical scholar at the University of Paris. He was among the early translators to render the New Testament from Latin into a vernacular language (in his case, French), and he urged that the illiterate be taught to read it. He has been called the *doyen* of French reformers for his anticipation, by perhaps five years, of some of Luther's ideas—though, like most intellectuals and nearly all humanists, he was to repudiate Luther in the end.

The most renowned of the humanists was Erasmus, a peripatetic scholar who was born in Rotterdam about 1466. The bastard son of a parish priest, Erasmus grew up to be the most urbane of 16th Century men, and his counsel was sought by popes and reformers, kings and scholars all over Europe.

No 16th Century man was more convinced of the need for reform than Erasmus; yet he was to remain within the fold of the Church. Well ahead of Luther, he took issue with the secular pursuits of the papacy, and he challenged the practices of fast-

ing, relic-worshiping, celibacy, indulgence-selling, pilgrimages, confession, the burning of heretics, and prayers to the saints. He went beyond Luther in urging the reduction of dogmas to as "few as possible, leaving opinion free on the rest."

Erasmus believed that education would change the world, and he expressed the wish that every plowboy might whistle the Psalms as he furrowed the soil. But education is a slow process. Erasmus addressed an intellectual elite; he himself judged the upheaval of revolution to be worse than the yoke of tyrants, and so he preferred not to upset the beliefs of the masses. Although he had a revolutionary mind, he was not a revolutionary at heart, and so he did not shake the world as Luther was to do.

As for Luther himself, for years all this talk of reform scarcely touched him, for he was preoccupied with his own salvation. But as a priest in Wittenberg, listening to the confessions of the people of the parish, he noticed with dismay how little remorse they had for their sins and how eagerly they sought to escape punishment. In addition, his acquaintance in the academic world was growing, and as it did his vista broadened. Gradually his personal quest for salvation and the talk of his contemporaries merged within him to foment a revolution.

The answer to the personal worries that plagued him came to Luther spectacularly. Studying the Scriptures in preparation for his lectures at the University of Wittenberg, he suddenly found in the Book of Romans the key he was looking for. It lay in a single word—the very word that had been his despair: *iustitia*, "justice," or "righteousness." Luther had associated the righteousness of God with His eternal condemnation of the damned. But studying at Wittenberg he fell upon a sentence of St. Paul, "The just shall live by faith," and in a flash the words took on a new meaning.

"Finally," Luther wrote, "God had mercy on me, and I began to understand that the righteousness of God is that gift of God by which a righteous man lives, namely, faith."

In other words, he concluded that the righteousness of God was not based on a disposition to condemn; it was based on mercy. The despair of Luther's life had been that he saw himself as undeserving of salvation. Now he was convinced that God gave, He did not buy and sell, and therefore grace was not purchasable.

Luther discerned support for his theory in the writings of St. Augustine, who 11 centuries before had written that the saved "are singled out not by their own merits, but by the grace of the Mediator; that is, they are justified . . . as by a free favor." These words cast light into the darkness of Luther's soul, giving him hope and courage.

Another word came into bold relief as Luther read still further. This was the word that the Latin Vulgate Bible rendered *poenitentia*, from the Greek *metanoia*. All the daunting associations of sin, guilt and penalty hung over the concept of "penitence," but *metanoia* could as legitimately be translated as "change of heart." To Luther that signified a state of mind in which man would turn to God in spontaneous good will. Regeneration of the soul, not retribution by a vengeful God, was the intention of the sacrament of Penance, he decided. And regeneration of the soul could not be earned; it had to come about through faith in God.

That was the start of Luther's theology, and when it crept into his lectures, nobody thought of it as new. But Luther had in fact brought about a revolutionary, practical approach to the abstruse discipline of theology. Luther was not himself a humanist, but he was influenced indirectly by humanistic ideas as they flowed into the mainstream of academic life; and his subjective view of man, though it was pious and northern, had a parallel in the views of the Renaissance humanists.

As energetically as he had previously tormented himself, now he labored to convey his ideas to others. His audiences grew, and the provincial University of Wittenberg grew, too. Luther slowly developed a modest fame.

Having questioned the concepts of righteousness and penance, Luther inevitably began to venture further afield. Soon he was speaking on other subjects. He began to criticize the worship of the saints, and then the trafficking in indulgences.

The subject of indulgences was already causing concern to others besides Luther, and this concern rose to a ground swell with the so-called St. Peter's indulgence of the early 1500s. Pope Julius II had ordered, long before his death, the erection of a new basilica over the tomb of St. Peter in the Vatican. To finance the undertaking he had issued a bull granting an indulgence to any who contributed toward its construction. His successor, Pope Leo X, reissued the indulgence bull for the continuation of the work.

Preachers campaigned throughout Europe, urging

the people to contribute to the project and making much of the benefits to be derived from the indulgences they would gain. Some of the preachers took license with Church doctrine; what they said was tantamount to promising that the mere purchase of this indulgence would assure the entrance into heaven not only of the donors, but also of their dead relatives who were suffering in purgatory.

There were many indulgence preachers all over Europe, but the most notable was one John Tetzel, a Dominican friar. He was a consummate salesman and a master showman, and his coming to town was something like the arrival of a circus. He was a great money-raiser for Rome, but an abomination to all serious men. In April of 1517 he set up a gaudy pulpit on the outskirts of Wittenberg.

On this occasion Tetzel was serving not only the Pope, but also the princely family of Hohenzollern, one of whose scions was Bishop of Halberstadt and Archbishop of Magdeburg and Mainz.

When the archbishopric of Mainz had recently become vacant, several wealthy men had sought the post, and Albert of Hohenzollern had won it by making the highest bid to Rome. To raise the fee, he and his family borrowed from the Fugger banking house of Augsburg, which arranged most of the financial transactions between the Curia and Germany. Albert therefore assumed the archbishopric of Mainz under a heavy debt.

When Leo X announced the renewal of the St. Peter's indulgence, rulers all over Europe protested that their national economies could not stand the outflow of gold to Rome. The Holy See, however, like all political powers, had ways of maneuvering to overcome such objections as this. Leo allowed Henry VIII to keep for the Royal Exchequer a fourth of the proceeds of the St. Peter's indulgence raised in England, and Francis I to retain a percentage of those raised in France. Against the receipts in Spain he lent a sum to King Charles I

(the future Emperor Charles V). And, in effect borrowing from Germany to ensure the payment of Albert of Hohenzollern's fee, Leo extended to the princely youth the royal privilege of taking one half the proceeds of his territory to put toward the payment of his debt to the Fugger bankers.

One ruler, Frederick the Wise of Saxony, was given no such concession as Albert and the monarchs of Europe. His recourse was to deny Tetzel admittance to Saxony. Tetzel got around the prohibition by establishing himself just outside the border, and the Wittenbergers streamed across to buy their indulgences.

Luther had no concern with Frederick's objections to Tetzel, but he deplored the Wittenbergers' gullible seeking after indulgences. In that era, when there were no journals in which to express opinions, it was customary practice for a scholar to post his ideas in some public place, and the door of the Castle Church served for such statements in Wittenberg. Aroused to indignation over Tetzel's circuslike performance, Luther summarized his ideas on the subject of indulgences in the form of 95 theses for debate, which he posted on a placard nailed to the north door of Frederick's Castle Church. The date was October 31, 1517.

Some of the theses were statements of definition; others posed questions. Anyone truly penitent, said Luther, would not whine to have punishment for his sins lifted, but rather would welcome it, as had Christ. Neither the Pope nor any man, he said, had jurisdiction over purgatory, and consequently the indulgence vendors who proclaimed indiscriminate release from purgatory were deceiving the people.

Furthermore, Luther asked, supposing the Pope possessed such powers as were imputed to him by the preachers of pardon; why then did he not in Christian charity empty purgatory forthwith? Why, since he was as rich as Croesus, did not the

Pope build St. Peter's basilica out of his own pocket instead of wringing those of the poor?

The public, which generally paid little heed to the academic debates of theologians, was electrified. Luther had touched on a tender subject, and the pent-up emotions of thousands resounded to his words. He had sent copies of the placard to a few friends; the friends circulated it among their friends, who passed it to printers, who sent it to Leipzig and Magdeburg almost overnight. By December the theses had reached Nuremberg, and in a few months they were all over Europe.

When Tetzel read Luther's theses he crowed: "Within three weeks I shall have the heretic thrown into the fire." Some of the Augustinians took alarm at the rising furor and begged Luther to desist. Luther, unwavering, decided instead to make certain that everyone knew exactly what he meant. He submitted a written treatise to his bishop, and to clear up any misunderstanding among the people he wrote a simplified version of his views in German. All over Germany men read these statements. The clamor rose, and he found himself hailed on the one side and slandered on the other.

The Archbishop Albert, seeing controversy brewing, called on Rome for advice and Tetzel urged the Curia to condemn Luther. But Pope Leo, who was a humanist and undisturbed by theological nitpicking, preferred not to make too much of what he regarded as a "monkish squabble." The Curia therefore took no immediate action.

Luther himself now poured forth treatises and pamphlets in great profusion, and he rapidly became a best-selling author. As excitement spread, the Curia began to take an interest. At last Luther was summoned to Rome. A political windfall saved him from going. The Elector Frederick, jealous of his territorial authority, was loath to have a Saxon subject leave German soil to be judged by Italians. The Pope had reasons for making concessions to

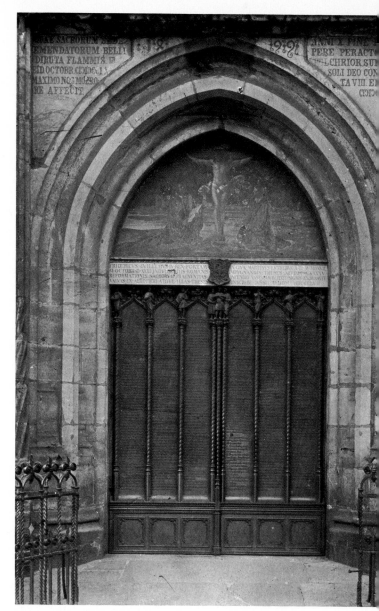

PORTALS OF PROTEST, *the doors of the Castle Church to which Luther nailed his famous 95 theses, were often used as a bulletin board by the townspeople of Wittenberg. The original wooden doors, damaged by fire, were replaced in 1858 by metal ones on which the theses are inscribed. The Crucifixion scene above the doors shows Luther and his disciple Melanchthon at the foot of the cross.*

Frederick, so he agreed to have his emissary in Germany examine Luther there.

In the fall of 1518, therefore, Luther journeyed to Augsburg to meet Cardinal Cajetan, General of the Dominican Order and an eminent theologian of the Curia. The Cardinal asked that Luther recant; Luther quoted Scripture in support of his belief that men were redeemed by faith and not by the purchase of indulgences. When Cajetan asserted that the theory on which indulgences rested was a matter of doctrine, Luther denied it. Cajetan finally lost patience and broke off the discussion.

The only result of the meeting was to push Luther into further heresy. Until Augsburg he had been willing to grant that the abuses in the Church existed without the Pope's knowledge, or at least without his connivance. From Augsburg he moved on to the conviction that the pontificate was a man-made fabrication, and that this lay at the root of a vicious perversion of the Christian faith.

In the summer of 1519 he went to debate his theology at Leipzig with John Eck, a champion of orthodoxy and a formidable speaker. Before a large audience, Eck accused Luther of holding a view similar to that of Jan Hus, a Bohemian scholar who had been burned at the stake 100 years before for urging men to cease depending on the sacraments and miracles and to seek God instead in Scripture. Luther stoutly replied that the Council of Constance had been wrong to condemn Hus; some of his ideas were thoroughly Christian. The assembly gasped in astonishment, for Luther was assaulting the theory that whatever power did not reside in the pope lay instead in a general council. If even a council could err, what authority was there left?

The growing storm might have prompted the Pope to act, but in the midst of it the Emperor Maximilian died. The Pope immersed himself in the politics of the Empire and found little time to spare for matters of heresy, so Luther was left alone for a time.

In August of 1520 he published an *Address to the Christian Nobility of the German Nation*, in which he declared that since the Church would not reform itself, it had therefore to be reformed by the secular authorities. Church and state had been intimately associated throughout the Christian era; they were considered to be the spiritual and temporal arms of divinely appointed rule—but the Church was considered to be the superior of the two. To suggest that the Church was remiss in its duty and should be taken in hand by the state was a revolutionary idea. It was to exert a decisive influence on the Reformation.

In October, Luther moved onto even more controversial ground. He published *The Babylonian Captivity of the Church*, a treatise that dealt mainly with the sacraments, or the religious rites, such as Baptism and Communion, through which, the Church taught, grace was conferred on the faithful by God. There were seven sacraments in all. They commemorated events recorded in the New Testament. Luther argued that in 1,000 years of captivity under Rome, the religion of Christ had been corrupted in faith, morals and ritual. Basing his judgment on his reading of the New Testament, Luther discarded the five sacraments that he could not find explicitly described there and retained only two—Baptism, which signified the washing away of original sin (the sin transmitted to man by the fall of Adam and Eve), and Communion, which commemorated Christ's sharing of bread and wine at the Last Supper with the 12 Apostles. In his earlier quarrels with the Church, Luther had been condemning practice; now he was attacking dogma. He was moving closer than he realized to an irreparable break with Rome.

In November came still another blow at the Church. In the *Treatise on Christian Liberty*, Luther declared that man was bound only to the law of the Word of God, and the Word of God was Scripture. From this it followed, in his view, that the clergy, though it had legitimate functions in administration and teaching, was not to be elevated above the rest of mankind, for all believers were priests. Luther prefaced this work with a conciliatory letter to Pope Leo X, making his last attempt to avoid a break with the Church, hoping instead that it would reform itself.

But in June the papacy had already acted. From his hunting lodge in the countryside near Rome, the Pope issued a bull condemning Luther's works and ordering them to be burned. Luther was given 60 days to recant or be excommunicated.

Rome had delayed too long. Luther's ideas had inflamed a nation, and the order met with obstruction all along the route to Wittenberg. Students rioted, burned anti-Lutheran publications instead of Luther's works, and threatened physical violence to the bearers of the bull.

Luther was no more daunted than the people. He responded with a blast headed *Against the Execrable Bull of Antichrist*, in which he declaimed: "[This] bull . . . is the sum of all impiety, blasphemy, ignorance, impudence, hypocrisy, lying—in a word, it is Satan and his Antichrist. . . . You, then, Leo X, you cardinals and the rest of you at Rome . . . I call upon you to renounce your diabolical blasphemy and audacious impiety, and, if you will not, we shall all hold your seat as possessed and oppressed by Satan, and the damned seat of Antichrist."

In the few cities where officials succeeded in burning Luther's books, they did it over the objections of solemn Germans. On December 10, 1520, Luther and the students at Wittenberg responded in kind. At a great bonfire before the city gate, Luther burned the *Canon Law*, the hallowed document that recorded the laws of the church.

Luther's excommunication followed. The only step that remained to be taken was the secular ban making Luther an outlaw of the land. In June of 1520 Charles V had succeeded Maximilian as Emperor. He called a diet, the assembly of the princes, prelates and representatives of the free cities. It convened at Worms in April 1521, and Luther was summoned before it.

The Diet of Worms was held against a backdrop of complex political forces—forces of which Luther was probably unaware, but over which he would not have troubled himself had he known of them. Rome, hoping that the Emperor would summarily condemn Luther, had sent two nuncios to the Diet. But the German constitution—which Charles had sworn in his coronation oath to uphold—declared that no German might be condemned for any crime without a trial. Charles, who was part Netherlander and part Spaniard, was a faithful son of the Church and might have liked to oblige the papacy, but he was advised that it would be unwise to go against the will of the German people.

As the members of the Diet assembled, Frederick the Wise and his chancellor tried to outmaneuver the papal nuncios and win the judges over to Luther's cause. Frederick had founded the University of Wittenberg, and he was proud of the eminence Luther had given it. Erasmus, who had no political aims but who applauded Luther's courage, worked to persuade other scholars and theologians to treat him fairly. Knights pledged their support, and threats circulated that the *Bundschuh*—the peasants, so named for the bound shoes they wore—would rise in rebellion if Luther was condemned.

When the Emperor and his retinue—which included the papal nuncios—arrived in Worms they found the city overwhelmingly on Luther's side. Poems, placards, pictures of him and stacks of his books appeared in the shops. One of the nuncios wrote to the Pope, "Nine tenths of the people are

DRESSED AS A KNIGHT, *Martin Luther towers symbolically over the city of Worms, where he was tried and condemned by the Church in 1521. He was then taken for his own safety to the fortress of Wartburg; while there he signed many of his letters "From the Isle of Patmos," after the Aegean island on which St. John is said to have written the Book of Revelations (hence the Latin words "In Pathmo" at the top of the woodcut). At right is the title page of the pope's "Bull against Martin Luther and Followers," which ordered his works to be burned.*

shouting 'Luther!' and the other tenth shouts 'Down with Rome!' "

Luther was given a trial, though it was not what he had anticipated. He had expected to be asked specific questions and to be given the chance to explain his views; instead he was shown 20 of his books piled on a bench and asked if he would recant the heresies they contained. He asked for time, was given a day, and returned the following evening to deliver a stirring statement that concluded: "Unless I am convicted by Scripture or by right reason . . . I neither can nor will recant anything, since it is neither right nor safe to act against conscience. God help me. Amen." He descended from the stand a hero to his champions.

The young Emperor, however, was tied by faith and by politics to Roman interests. After a day of reflection he summoned his counselors and told them, "A single friar who goes counter to all Christianity for 1,000 years must be wrong. . . . Therefore, I am resolved to stake my lands, my friends, my body, my life and my soul [to defend the Church of Rome]." A month later he issued the Edict of Worms, declaring Luther an outlaw. The Elector Frederick, fearing for Luther's safety, thereupon arranged to have him taken to a mountain fortress, the Wartburg, where he remained in hiding for the better part of a year.

But neither the Edict of Worms nor Luther's seclusion could stem the tide that now swept over Germany. The Reformation was underway, and neither prelates nor statesmen could halt it. Luther had brought into open debate all manner of issues against the Church; he had for four years now been writing steadily on the nature of faith and the sacraments; the function and performance of the Mass; on marriage, holidays, and fasting. Other men took up these ideas while he was in the Wartburg and put some of them into practice. Bodenstein von Carlstadt, a priest and professor at

Wittenberg—the man who had conferred the doctorate on Luther some 10 years before—began to make changes in worship and teaching. On Christmas Day of 1521 he celebrated the Mass for the first time without clerical vestments and spoke throughout in German.

Other changes were instituted. Fast days and confession were abolished. Priests began to marry, and so did monks. "Good heavens," said Luther, hearing that monks were taking wives. "Monks too? They'll never give me one." (Some four years later he changed his mind and married a former nun.)

While he remained in hiding, Luther translated the New Testament, a monumental undertaking. As literature his translation bears comparison with the King James version in English. More than any other single work, Luther's Bible was to establish modern vernacular German.

He approved the orderly changes that took place in his absence, but soon the situation took a turn toward violence, and that caused him consternation. Students rioted and desecrated churches and their altars. Luther himself, for all his cocky invective, could not countenance violence, and he returned to Wittenberg at the request of the town council to help restore order.

A transformation had taken place in him during his stay in the Wartburg. He had grown a beard and a full head of hair (he had formerly been tonsured). He had taken on flesh and poise. He took charge of Wittenberg and in a few days had returned the town to peace. The power of his personality was to dominate Wittenberg for another 25 years, as long as he lived.

His battles were not yet over, for he did not anticipate that the Scripture he read so unequivocally would be read in other ways by other men. But Luther had precipitated reform where other men had tried and failed for more than a century.

Why Martin Luther? Few of his ideas were new; most had been raised or suggested by a host of earlier theologians—John Wycliffe in 14th Century England; Jan Hus in 14th Century Bohemia; a Dominican friar, Savonarola, in Florence only a generation before Luther; Lefèvre in France and Erasmus internationally in Luther's own time. Elements of all their ideas were to be found in the doctrine at which Luther eventually arrived, though Luther did not consciously take them as his models.

Some of his forerunners had failed because they looked back, not forward, and tried to restore a view of life that was outdated. Some were ahead of their times, and cried out in vain because people were not ready to listen. Others appeared in nations in which either the Church was so much in control (as in Italy) that it could overrule the wishes of a few, or the state was so strong (as in England) that it offset interference from Rome.

Luther, on the other hand, appeared at a decisive moment of history, in a propitious time and place. Instead of going against the current, he rode an epochal tidal wave. He addressed a nation that more than any other in Europe wished to detach itself from Rome; and he spoke not to the intellectual elite, as Erasmus did, but to the people, and in language they could understand. Thanks to the fortune of Luther's timing and to his remarkable facility with language, Germany became the theater of a religious conflict that was to sweep through all of Europe in less than half a century.

Though the Emperor Charles V remained true to his faith, he did not subdue the rebellious princes of the Empire. In 1556 he abdicated his throne and went to Spain to die in a monastery. Behind him in Germany the princes assumed the right to regulate the Church in their territories—and they made the Church Lutheran. Not all the princes went over to the Reformation, but the universal character of medieval religion was broken, never to be restored.

A YOUTHFUL SELF-PORTRAIT *was drawn by the talented Dürer when he was only 13 years old.*

DURER: DRAFTSMAN OF THE SPIRIT

As the thunderclouds of the Reformation piled up over Germany, one artist, Albrecht Dürer, captured on paper all the fears, the fantasies and the religious fervor of his troubled land. During his lifetime Dürer tried to imbue the Gothic spirit of medieval times with the new Renaissance belief in the dignity of man. An exacting draftsman, he produced an array of inspired paintings and a brilliant range of woodcuts and engravings, which were reproduced by the thousands on newly developed printing presses. He was, and remains, Germany's most popular artist—the man who represented the soul of his nation on the eve of reform.

A Fresh Awareness of Man's Foibles and Fate

Albrecht Dürer was born in Nuremberg in 1471, the third of 18 children of a Hungarian goldsmith. Apprenticed to his father's craft, he had already gained an eye for solidity and detail when at the age of 15 he began his tutelage under Michael Wolgemut, the most important painter in Nuremberg. Soon young Dürer was an accomplished artist and engraver, chiefly of popular religious themes.

Two philosophies conflicted in Dürer's art. In part it mirrored the Gothic mysticism of the day, which was fraught with heavy religious symbolism, romantic legends of brave knights and an obsession with the Devil and the Day of Judgment—a day Dürer feared all his life. But it was also filled with a restless striving for a new, individual approach toward faith and the meaning of life. Dürer rejoiced in the world around him. He drew people and places as they were, right down to the warts on chins and the bark on trees, and through this realism brought fresh insights to the nature of man.

MAN'S NOBILITY *is personified by this German on a horse in Dürer's engraving, the "Knight, Death and Devil." Like a true Christian, the rider ignores both Death, seen as a corpse holding an hourglass, and the Devil, who carries a pike and wears a boar's head and bat's wings. At lower left is the monogram with which Dürer signed much of his work.*

MAN'S FOLLY *is illustrated in these woodcuts for Sebastian Brant's book of satirical verse, "Ship of Fools." At upper right an addled jester puts out his neighbor's fire while his own house burns. At lower left a foolish boatman tends his sail while his ship breaks up beneath him. The other two prints show trusting souls talking to geese and swine.*

"APOLLO AND DIANA," an engraving done in 1505, after a journey to Italy, shows Dürer's genius for drawing the human form. For practice, he often attended public baths in Germany to sketch the lightly clad bathers there, and in the process introduced the classic nude to German art.

"THE BATTLE OF THE SEA GODS" is drawn after an

A Classicist in Germany

The Italian Renaissance came into full flower in Dürer's lifetime, and he almost singlehandedly transported its qualities across the Alps in an attempt to infuse them into German art. As a youth he sharpened his drawings by copying the works of Antonio Pollaiuolo and Mantegna; when he was 23 he went

...ngraving by the Italian master Andrea Mantegna. Such skillful exercises helped Dürer gain a Renaissance mastery of form, composition and perspective.

to Venice on the first of a pair of trips to Italy to see how the masters there painted and thought. Like many of the Renaissance giants, Dürer studied anatomy and classical statuary assiduously, in order to draw the human body with deft precision. One of his greatest delights, as with other artists who sought their ideals of beauty in classic forms, was the detailed re-creation of heroic themes from Greek mythology. Some of these portrayed titanic struggles like the one shown above—battles that in some ways foreshadowed the later torments of the Reformation and of Dürer's own troubled soul.

A Divine Passion Revealed through a Common Faith

As his countrymen struggled to understand the relationship between God and man, Dürer tried to free religious art from its Gothic formalism and make it vividly human. His illustrations of traditional New Testament episodes were set in everyday German surroundings and the faces were often those of solid German burghers and peasants; their expressions revealed a new warmth and dignity.

Like many of his subjects, Dürer keenly felt the stirrings of the Reformation. He was an ardent admirer of Luther, and was concerned at what he felt were the excesses of the Church. But Dürer was an artist and observer, not a theological crusader. Unable to give up his deep-rooted Church training, he remained a Catholic until he died.

"THE PRODIGAL SON" among the swine was portrayed by Dürer as an agonized figure, symbolic of Germans trying to reach a new relationship with God. The setting is a crumbling German farm.

"THE FOUR HORSEMEN" of the Apocalypse (left) trample their victims in
Dürer's woodcut depicting the end of
the world. Death rides a skeletal nag,
Want swings his scales, Sickness
lifts a sword and War aims his arrow.

A BATTLE IN HEAVEN rages above
landscape of Germany in "St. Mich
Fighting the Dragon." St. Micha
like Siegfried of German mythol
—thrusts his lance at the drago
throat while warriorlike angels ass

Fearful Visions of Evil and Good

Dürer shared with his countrymen the dread ex-
pectation that the end of the world was close at
hand. Plague and disease ravaged the population,
bad harvests bred famines and peasants had started to revolt against their lords. The air was rife
with religious anarchy as the very structure of the
Church swayed under the attacks of the reformers.

Dürer's mind was filled with the confusion of
his times, and his nights were haunted by fantasies. "How often do I see great art in my sleep," he
wrote, "but waking cannot recall it." Yet some of
his dreams were transformed into works of violent power (above and right) which both portrayed
and anticipated the religious upheaval of his age.

3

LEADERS OF THE PROTEST

While Luther remained hidden in the Wartburg, other men were busy carrying his ideas—and new ones—to conclusions he had not foreseen. The result was a splitting of Christendom into several denominations that came to be known generally as the Reformed Churches. Many men contributed to the movement; three were to stamp its development as decisively as Luther had stamped its beginning. In Luther the Reformation had had a prophet; it was to have an executor in a Swiss, Ulrich Zwingli; a lawmaker in a Frenchman, John Calvin; and an apostle in a Scot, John Knox.

The first people to develop the ideas generated by Luther were the Swiss, who were by language kindred to, but by temperament and politics distinct from, the Germans.

The Swiss were a physically sturdy and mentally resourceful people, and by 16th Century standards they were singularly independent. To survive the hardships of the cold and rugged Alpine terrain required not only stamina, but also a harnessing of individual ingenuity to group cooperation. At various times foreign rulers had made attempts to control Switzerland, but time and again the clever and hardy Swiss had defeated them. Repeated rebuffs of foreign interference had inspired a fervent patriotism that by the 16th Century was an important part of the Swiss national character.

The territory now called Switzerland was a confederation of 13 cantons, or states, that had a remarkable degree of democracy. The land was nominally part of the Holy Roman Empire, but the Confederation governed its own affairs. The cantons had a common legislative body for dealing with foreign affairs; and each canton had several councils for regulation of its own affairs. Most of the representatives served by election, but some assemblies consisted of the entire male citizenry. And just as they were independent of emperors and dukes, so the Swiss were largely independent of the popes. The same city and canton councils that governed civic affairs also supervised the activities of the clergy and taxed Church property, and even the bishops were bound by their laws.

Whereas other countries had a series of social classes extending downward from monarch to serfs, Switzerland had only two classes: the bourgeoisie,

EARLY PROTESTANTS, *among them Martin Luther (far left) and Ulrich Zwingli, the great Swiss reformer (right, in cap), appear to be shielded by John Frederick the Magnanimous, Elector of Saxony (center) in this group portrait painted about 1530. The Saxon ruling family stanchly protected Luther from Roman wrath and, by extension, supported the entire Reformation.*

who lived in the cities that had sprung up where merchants stopped in the mountain passes en route across the Continent, and the free peasants, who made their living by shepherding and dairy farming. There was some conflict of interest between the cities and the Forest Cantons—and this was to make itself felt in religious terms—but in foreign affairs the Swiss national patriotism generally superseded local differences.

The most advanced city of the Confederation was Zurich. Situated on a tributary of the Rhine and at an opening in the mountains, it shared in the river and overland commerce between Germany and Italy. Lying near Basel, where a distinguished university nourished humanism and a center of printing turned out books that vied with those of Renaissance Italy, it was the beneficiary of new ideas. Some of the priests there had for years been preaching against indulgences and corruption of morals. Into this city, in 1519, came a new priest in the person of Ulrich Zwingli.

Zwingli was born January 1, 1484—less than two months after Luther—in a gabled cottage of oak beams and mullioned windows that still stands in Wildhaus, a snowbound hamlet high in the mountains of the canton of St. Gall. He received his early education under the tutelage of an uncle who was a parish priest. At an early age he showed a flair for music; he learned to play half a dozen instruments well, and he had so good a voice that a group of Dominican monks tried to enlist him for their choir. When he was 10 he was sent away to a school in Basel, where he promptly distinguished himself for his brightness. He later studied at Bern, and at the Universities of Vienna and Basel, where humanists taught him to value the classics and scorn ecclesiastical corruption.

Zwingli was ordained in 1506, when he was 22, and for a time he served as a parish priest in small villages. At 29 he began to learn Greek in order to read the New Testament in the original. At 35, having acquired some fame as a speaker, he was appointed to the cathedral at Zurich—and there, in 1519, he embarked on a career as a reformer.

Without consciously challenging the Church as Luther had done, Zwingli set about trying to raise the moral standards of his congregation—preaching against the sale of indulgences and the veneration of saints, encouraging an acquaintance with the Scriptures and urging simplicity of ritual. He seems to have arrived at his ideas through the influence of humanism and not through that of Luther, though at about this time he discovered the writings of the Wittenberger and arranged to have several hundred copies of Luther's works distributed among the people of Switzerland. Later he was to object when people called him "Lutheran," and to aver he had been preaching the Gospel "before anyone in our region had ever heard of Luther."

Zwingli agreed with much of Luther's doctrine, but he was far more rigorous in its application. He dispensed with all pageantry and, taking literally the Second Commandment, "Thou shalt not make unto thee any graven image," he discarded all the implements of ritual—not only crucifixes and statuary, but chalices, censers and clerical vestments as well. He never lost his love of music (he is said to have calmed a class of obstreperous boys once by playing on the lute); but because he could find no authority in Scripture for liturgical music, he removed even the organ from the church and banned the singing of hymns.

These measures caused no iconoclastic riots in Zurich, as they did elsewhere; the removal of statuary and the modification of laws proceeded under the orderly supervision of the civil authorities. The Bishop of Constance, hearing of Zwingli's innovations, urged him to desist, but the council of Zurich supported Zwingli, and so did his fellow priests. And the Pope seems to have learned a les-

IN INDIA, AN ERA OF TOLERANCE

While Catholics and Protestants in Europe were conducting holy wars and purges, India was entering a time of remarkable religious toleration under the reign of Akbar, greatest of the Mogul emperors (seen here in a contemporary sketch).

For centuries India had been the scene of bitter feuds between Hindus, Moslems, Jains, Buddhists and Parsees. Then in 1526 the armies of the Moguls—descendants of the fierce Mongol tribesmen who had ravaged Asia under Genghis Khan—crossed over the mountains from Afghanistan and conquered the Sultanate of Delhi in the Ganges Valley. Within two generations, Akbar, the grandson of the first conqueror, had subjugated most of India.

Though raised an orthodox Moslem, Akbar believed, as one awed chronicler reported, "that there were sensible men in all religions." He built a special house of worship where he could listen to debates among philosophers and holy men from

every sect in India. (Even visiting Jesuits joined in, but their zeal often irked the other participants.) In the end Akbar, like many a dissatisfied European reformer, founded his own sect. A mélange of many beliefs, it enjoyed only limited popularity and disappeared soon after his death.

son from the loss of so many Germans through his treatment of Martin Luther; hoping not to lose the Swiss as well, he let Zwingli alone.

If the Zurichers accepted Zwinglian measures readily and the Pope overlooked them, the man who had started reform did not. Luther himself, now that he had broken with the Church, had withdrawn into conservatism. He had restored some of the traditional ideas he had once discarded, and the service performed in Lutheran churches was similar to that of the Roman Church, except that the language was German instead of Latin. But Zwinglian ideas filtered into Germany, and in places they began to supersede Lutheran ideas and practices.

Once this process began, Luther engaged in pamphlet warfare with Zwingli. The followers of both men grew truculent, and soon the partisans of reform began to fear that the schism would mean an end for them all. In an endeavor to achieve unity,

Philip of Hesse, an ambitious young prince, invited Luther and Zwingli to a colloquy at his castle at Marburg in the fall of 1529. Here the two reformers at last confronted each other.

Both men assumed the infallibility of Scripture, but each was intransigent about the interpretation of it. Luther, who was essentially mystical, interpreted the Bible literally—or, as he expressed it, by faith; Zwingli, who shared the humanists' esteem for the intellect and aimed for a practical religion, interpreted the Bible by reason. Luther had by now taken the view that the body and blood of Christ were miraculously present in the bread and wine served at Communion; Zwingli held that the rite was simply a symbolic commemoration of the Last Supper. The two men tried hard to come to agreement, but they reached an impasse over this question.

They ended the meeting, as they had begun, in disagreement. Notwithstanding, Zwingli offered to shake hands in an expression of amity, but Luther indignantly refused. He later compared Zwingli to the Apostle Judas betraying Christ, and pontificated: "I will not let the devil teach me anything in my church."

After he returned from Marburg, Zwingli devoted much of his time to writing, and to serving, through his influence over the city council, as virtual governor of Zurich. His rule was stern and his attitude toward opposition uncompromising, but he nevertheless remained a humanist at heart. Though he sanctioned persecution of heretics (because they menaced civil order), he was broadminded enough to avow that paradise would welcome admirable Jews and pagans; he once wrote that "there has not been any good man . . . from the very beginning of the world even to its end, whom you will not see [in paradise] with God." This was a rare attitude among reformers, and Luther for one concluded that Zwingli was a heathen.

Among the Swiss generally, Zwingli's practices were readily adopted in the urban areas, but he had to face opposition from the Forest Cantons. These were in the interior Alps, most of them off the trade routes; they were conservative, and they held to the Catholic faith. The religious split threatened to destroy the Confederation. Five cantons formed a Catholic League, and in 1531, after two years of growing dissension, sent an army of 8,000 men against Zurich.

Zwingli mustered 1,500 soldiers, donned a helmet and led the Zurichers in battle. The odds were too great. Zwingli was felled by a pike, and most of his troops were slain or scattered. At nightfall plunderers scavenging the field by torchlight found him under a pear tree, still alive, and slew him. The Reformation had lost perhaps its most humane leader.

The focus of reform now shifted to Geneva and the stern soul of John Calvin. Calvin was born in 1509 in Noyon, a cathedral city in Picardy, in northern France, where his father was employed as notary for the diocese. Even as a child he showed a remarkable precision of mind and a consuming urge for perfection. He made harsh demands of others and of himself, yet his schoolmates are said to have liked him.

Expecting to become a priest, Calvin went to Paris to study theology and Scholastic philosophy —a subject that must have been congenial to his exacting mind. Midway in his studies for the priesthood, however, he was suddenly sent by his father to study law at Orléans. Like Luther's father, the elder Calvin envisioned his son in a profession of money and rank. John was never to practice law, but he was always to regard law as the outstanding achievement of mankind. At Orléans he studied under some humanists, but the prevailing humanistic idea, that worldly pleasure was honorable, seems to have escaped him; instead, what seems to have impressed him most in the classics was the spirit of Stoicism—the Greek philosophy that exalted discipline and preached impassivity in the face of pleasure and pain. Never in the philosophy he formulated did he pay homage to Stoicism as such, but discipline and impassivity were to be fundamental to the Calvinist creed. While at Orléans, Calvin also fell under the spell of evangelical literature and began consorting with reformers.

France in the 1530s was an uncertain place for men of unorthodox views; King Francis I shifted between toleration and persecution of heretics, according to political considerations. In the fall of 1534 he was on the offensive; the new faith was being equated with violence and lawlessness. Calvin, fearing that he might be arrested for his association with reformers, left France for Basel.

In Basel he undertook to write *The Institutes of the Christian Religion*, which was both a defense of the reform movement and a textbook for instruction. It was to exert a powerful influence on the Reformation—more powerful even than any single work of Luther's. It was the first significant comprehensive and logical exposition of reform beliefs, and in it Calvin went further than Luther in revising medieval conceptions of religious law. And it was far more somber than the writings of Luther. Whereas Luther had envisioned God as eminently merciful and attacked the Church practices that obscured that view, Calvin conceived a God whose most significant aspect was His absolute sovereignty. Turning to the Old Testament for much of his inspiration, Calvin depicted a Jehovah far more forbidding than the God of Luther.

If the concept behind the *Institutes* was formidable, the book itself was a lucid, logical, systematic statement of reform beliefs, and it captured the imagination of hundreds of thousands. Besides the Old Testament, it drew from early Church writers—mainly St. Paul and St. Augustine, who figured largely in both Catholic and Lutheran thinking; from medieval Scholastic theologians; and from Luther and Zwingli. There were no original ideas in the book; Calvin synthesized the views of centuries of writers who preceded him.

Not surprisingly, considering Calvin's reverence for the law, the *Institutes* began with an exposition of the Ten Commandments. It went on to deal with creed, and it drew from the same creed used by the Church of Rome, affirming belief in a trinitarian God, the divinity of Christ and resurrection after death. On the question of salvation Calvin differed with both Luther and the Catholic Church. Luther had denied the Church's stand that salvation could be merited by good works; he made it dependent on faith alone. Calvin reduced this principle to a "doctrine of the elect," by which only the chosen of God were saved. Next Calvin took up the sacraments, accepting Baptism and the Lord's Supper and discarding the other five.

Finally—and most significant for the course the

Reformation was to take—the *Institutes* dealt with the relationship between church and state. On this Calvin disavowed the accusations of lawlessness that were being leveled against reformers, saying that "man is the subject of two kinds of government," the civil law and the rule of God, that the "civil government is designed . . . to establish general peace and tranquillity," and that "it is impossible to resist the magistrate without at the same time resisting God Himself."

But to this exaltation of the civil law Calvin added significant qualifications. He asserted that when Moses led the Jews against the king of Egypt he was "armed with authority from Heaven [and] punished an inferior power by a superior one. . . . The correction of tyrannical domination is the vengeance of God," he wrote, and the obedience due to the civil government ought "not to seduce us from obedience to Him to whose will the desires of all kings ought to be subject." These were subtle words from a man whose creed was centered in law. They were to travel all over Europe and set the Continent afire with political revolution that would rage for the rest of the century.

But that was still in the future. After publishing the *Institutes* Calvin set off for Strasbourg, where he intended to devote himself to writing and study. En route he stopped in Geneva, meaning only to stay for the night; instead he remained, except for one absence of a few years, for the rest of his life. At Geneva he put into practice a theocratic regime and exercised a personal domination such as few men have ever achieved.

Geneva in the 1530s was a wealthy center of trade and manufacture, and a republic independent of the Swiss Confederation. Independence here was newer than elsewhere in Switzerland; Geneva had only recently thrown off the yoke of the dukes of Savoy, and it had been ruled as part of an area that today belongs to France. Like the cantons of

CALVIN'S "BLUE LAWS" FOR INNS

If any one blasphemes the name of God or says, "By the body, 'sblood, zounds" or anything like, or who gives himself to the devil or uses similar execrable imprecations, he shall be punished.

If any one insults any one else the host shall deliver him up to justice.

The host shall be obliged to report to the government any insolent or dissolute acts committed by the guests.

The host shall be obliged to keep in a public place a French Bible, in which any one who wishes may read.

[He] shall not allow any dissoluteness like dancing, dice or cards, nor receive any one suspected of being a debauché.

He shall not allow indecent songs.

Nobody shall be allowed to sit up after nine o'clock at night except informers.

Switzerland, Geneva governed itself by town assemblies, and these had jurisdiction over ecclesiastical as well as civil affairs. The people, however, were boisterous and undisciplined, heady with their new-won freedom and suspicious of foreigners. Their faith was an amorphous combination of Lutheran and Zwinglian ideas, and the most prominent preacher was a red-bearded Frenchman, William Farel, a man of such fiery disposition that a friend had to remind him that a preacher ought to teach rather than curse.

Farel had studied at the University of Paris, where he had come under the influence of French humanists. Like his masters, he had hoped for reform within the Church; despairing of it, he left France to wander through Europe as an independent preacher. On and off since 1532 he had been in Geneva and he mourned that the city had no leader to tame the roistering people. When Calvin arrived, Farel saw in his earnestness a stanch spirit capable of reforming the licentiousness that prevailed in Geneva. He exhorted Calvin to stay; Calvin demurred; Farel threatened him with the curse of God if he refused. Calvin stayed.

Together they set about establishing an austere regime in Geneva. They put strictures on gambling, drinking, singing and dancing, and ordered transgressors exiled. But the Genevese were not ready for such austerity as Calvin's, and both men were themselves exiled by an angry city council. A few years later the council had second thoughts and recalled Calvin; it appeared to the council not only that morals were going to ruin, but that the reform movement was losing to Catholicism and that the lack of discipline was making Geneva vulnerable to renewed threats from Savoy.

When Calvin returned his first action was to persuade the city council to appoint a commission of five clergymen and six lay councilors, with himself as its head, to draw up a legislative code. The result was the *Ecclesiastical Ordinances*, a constitution for the Reformed Church, which was to be supported by the state. It divided the Church into a hierarchy of pastors and teachers (clergymen), plus elders and deacons (laymen). New pastors, in order to preach, needed the authorization of the incumbent pastors, the magistrates and, in theory, the congregation.

Here was the first application of democracy to ecclesiastical affairs. But this democracy, like Calvin's words against the secular state, was subtle; actually the congregation took little part. Participation by laymen would not come until later, when other men expanded on Calvin as he had expanded on Luther and Zwingli. The law was the Bible; the pastors were the interpreters of the law; and the civil government was obliged to enforce that law as the pastors interpreted it.

The constitution also provided for a Consistory, or Presbytery, composed of five pastors and 12 elders. Calvin had no official post in the Consistory, but he dominated it nonetheless. The Consistory determined the worship and oversaw the moral conduct of every citizen of Geneva. It sent an elder to inspect every house at least once a year; it might at any time summon any member of the congregation to account for his actions; and it might excommunicate offenders. Excommunication denied the sinner participation in the Lord's Supper (the Communion rite, in which bread and wine were passed to the faithful) and forbade other citizens to associate with him—though he was expected to attend sermons for his enlightenment all the same. If he had not mended his ways in six months he was exiled from the city. Calvin was to rule this theocracy for 23 years, until his death, and it was a rule that knew no mercy.

But Calvin drove himself as mercilessly as he drove his congregation. He preached frequent sermons, sometimes as many as four a week, and all the citizens were expected to attend, save only the few excused to tend children or cattle. He carried on a prodigious correspondence with theologians far and wide. He wrote dozens of books and tracts, and revised his *Institutes* five times in 20 years. When he was done he had left no detail of doctrine or individual conduct unprescribed.

The people of Geneva, who were so proud of having overthrown the rule of Savoyard dukes and Roman prelates, submitted willingly to a tyranny far harsher and all-embracing. A few rash citizens who hated the theocrat called him Cain and named their dogs Calvin; but dissenters paid for their sins with their lives or eviction—Calvin was as harsh as Luther and the Church of Rome in regarding opposition as the handiwork of the devil and in suppressing heresy. And influential citizens kept him going; Swiss independence had been born of discipline, and most of the Swiss took discipline for granted. Furthermore, Calvin's doctrine of the elect flattered their vanity; for a people already steeped in patriotism, it was a short step to the proud belief that they were the chosen of God.

Calvin's rule extended into every phase of society. He introduced sanitary regulations that gave Geneva a cleanliness and neatness for which it is noted to this day. He persuaded the city council to finance new industry. He founded the Genevan Academy (later to be the University of Geneva) to train men for the ministry.

Though he employed the civil government to effect Church measures, Calvin never invoked nationalism; hence his creed was better able to travel than either Luther's or Zwingli's. And travel it did. Graduates of his academy went out all over Europe, carrying Calvin's influence beyond the Alps, the Rhine and the North Sea, as far away as Scotland. And here his teachings were taken up by another man, who was to graft Calvinism onto the Scottish soul—and in the bargain to transform the social and political organization of an undeveloped nation.

Scotland in the 16th Century lagged far behind the major countries of Europe politically and economically. It was ruled for much of the time by Mary of Lorraine, who as the widow of James V served as regent during the minority of her daughter, the future Mary Queen of Scots. Mary of Lorraine was French and Catholic (she was a sister of the Duke of Guise, who was political leader of the Catholics in France and whose heir was to vie with Henry IV for the French throne). During her time distaste for the French mounted, and so did distaste for the clergy, as bishops and priests exacted heavy dues from the people. Power was largely in the hands of feudal barons, whom former rulers of Scotland had never succeeded in subduing.

The land was as badly off economically as it was politically. It had few cities and these were small; therefore it had little commerce and industry. Even most of the soil was poor, so the peasant had a harder lot than elsewhere.

But Scotland had fertile soil of another kind. Respect for old ways was breaking down, and new ideas were filtering in. In this promising ground a Calvinist-inspired itinerant preacher, John Knox, was to sow the seeds of Reformation.

Knox was a Scottish peasant born in the county of East Lothian. A peasant who hobnobbed with monarchs and barons, he was to take the doctrine of the elect, which Calvin had addressed primarily to a patrician bourgeoisie, and give it to a people who were rooted in the earth.

The date of his birth is uncertain, but it was probably about 1514. Except that he was ordained a priest, almost nothing is known of his life until 1546, when he was associating with reformers in the town of St. Andrews.

In June of 1547, St. Andrews was besieged by the French fleet, which had been called in by Mary of Lorraine to put down insurgents who had seized a cardinal's residence. Several reformers were captured, including Knox, who spent the next 19 months in chains on a ship on the Loire River.

When he was released he went to England for five years, where he won such fame for himself that he was appointed preacher to the royal court. With the accession to the throne of Mary Tudor, who tried to restore an already displaced Catholicism to England, he was obliged to leave. Next he traveled through Europe for several years, meeting reformers in Frankfurt, Dieppe, Geneva and elsewhere, but maintaining a correspondence with friends at home who were now agitating seriously for reform.

The Scottish nobles had in the meantime drawn together in a "Common Band." Calling themselves the "Lords of the Congregation of Jesus Christ," they demanded "that it be lawful to use ourselves in matters of religion and conscience as we must answer to God." Meeting with resistance from the regent, they found they needed a leader to organize their movement. Remembering Knox, they sent word to him in Geneva, asking him to come back and assist their cause. He came in May of 1559.

Though it was on the invitation of the nobles that he came, Knox's message was directed at the populace. The reform he instituted, modeled on Calvin's Geneva, gave laymen a voice in the affairs of the Church. The common people, who had previously been of little account in Scotland, began to emerge as a political and social force; in fact, the organization of the Church raised a new class out of the lower bourgeoisie. An Englishman, hearing of this development, was moved to exclaim, "God keep us from such visitation as Knox hath attempted in Scotland: the people to be orderers of things!"

And indeed, before they learned to manage themselves responsibly, the people caused considerable disorder. Fired by Knox's preaching against idolatry and his reminders of "what commandment God had given for the destruction of the monuments there-

A HISTORIC CONFRONTATION, *the trial of Mary Queen of Scots marked the end of years of intrigue between Mary, a Catholic, and her cousin Elizabeth, the Protestant Queen of England. Accused of conspiring to assassinate Elizabeth, Mary (A) was tried by a court of English nobility, among them the Lord Chancellor (1), the Earl of Oxford (3) and Sir Francis Walsingham (28). She was executed in 1587.*

of," the multitudes destroyed images and razed churches, pillaged monasteries and assaulted priests. Riots occurred wherever Knox preached—in Perth, Edinburgh, St. Andrews—culminating in civil war.

Mary of Lorraine again tried to put down the rebellion with armed force; and the future Mary Queen of Scots, living in Paris as the wife of King Francis II, sent troops from France. The Lords of the Congregation formed a league with Queen Elizabeth of England, who sent troops that put an end to the civil war. Later they signed the Treaty of Edinburgh, which secured the independence of Scotland against England and France alike.

Soon after these negotiations the largest Parliament yet to convene in Scottish history assembled to consider the religious question. Hundreds of small nobles and bourgeoisie turned out who had never bothered to come before. They called on Knox to draw up a confession of faith; he did, and based it on the Calvinist creed. Parliament then passed laws abolishing the pope's authority and forbidding Catholic rites. It made the maintenance of religion the duty of the state, and provided for the payment of ministers by the government.

This was the situation that greeted Mary Queen of Scots when she arrived to ascend the throne in 1561. Having been brought up in France during her mother's regency in Scotland, she was French and Catholic in temperament and in outlook.

In 1561 Mary was 18 and already a widow. She was tall, beautiful, high-spirited and ambitious. She came from the most luxurious court in Europe to a bleak land where her religion was outlawed, her Gallic style distasteful to a dour people, and her power curtailed by commoners whom she held in contempt. She bungled her relations with the Scots and had a tragic reign.

Knox was preaching in Edinburgh when Mary landed, and Mary sent for him, hoping to tame the rabble-rouser. They had five interviews, in which, according to Knox's account, there was on Mary's part so much "womanly weeping . . . that her chamberboy could scarce get napkins enough to dry her eyes." He informed Mary that "right religion took . . . authority [not] from worldly princes but from the Eternal God alone"—meaning, of course, from himself as spokesman.

Two unpopular marriages, scandal, court intrigue and a murder for which the Queen was blamed (probably rightly) led eventually to Mary's being deposed by Parliament—and, by extension, to the final disgrace of Catholicism. The son Mary left behind when she fled was brought up a Protestant; he and Parliament and Knox together settled Calvinism in Scotland forever.

The Scots under Knox and Mary's son, James VI, had no freedom of worship—in theory the penalties for holding Catholic rites were confiscation of property, exile or death—but there was so little resistance to the Reformed Church that there was no persecution to speak of. Despite the earlier iconoclastic riots, the Reformation in Scotland was the least bloody of any in Europe.

Much blood was yet to be spilled elsewhere, however. Without exception the very reformers who won their own freedom by challenging established order would brook no opposition from others. To them, as to the Catholic Church they scorned, dissent meant heresy, and they countered heresy with persecution.

The worst of the persecution was visited on the Anabaptists, adherents of various offshoots of the reform movement. Anabaptism, which means literally "baptizing anew," was a catch-all name given to different groups that practiced adult baptism. The Church of Rome and the major reformers administered baptism to infants.

According to the beliefs of some Anabaptists, no Christian could take part in a secular state, because the secular state was sinful; thus the Anabaptists seemed to others subversive of everything that held society together. A few Anabaptists were radical anarchists, but most were orderly—and, interestingly, the Anabaptists were the only religious group in that intolerant era who ever made freedom of worship a tenet of their creed.

The first Anabaptists arose in Zurich in 1525, and others sprang up elsewhere, some independently, some inspired by refugees. Wherever they went they met with persecution, whether the prevailing faith was Lutheran, Calvinist or Catholic. Their survivors wandered all over Europe. Some eventually found haven in Moravia and Poland; others finally came to the American Colonies. The Amish and the Mennonites in Pennsylvania and the Middle West are descendants of the Anabaptist movement, and even today they seclude themselves from the world that surrounds their communities. In the 16th Century the Anabaptists' eccentricities were so unsettling that the major reformers would never admit that such a mutation had sprung from their own roots.

But the Anabaptists were a variant. The Reformation proper was carried by men more attuned to the spirit of the times—men of whom Luther, Zwingli, Calvin and Knox were the spokesmen. Their ideas varied, but they all held these principles in common: reliance on Scripture, justification by faith, and repudiation of rule from Rome. Where they differed was in national heritage and prevailing politics. They had challenged the Church of Rome not only because of its corruption, nor only because corruption had become confused with doctrine, but because national states were emerging. A struggle for power therefore ensued in which secular men wrestled with ecclesiastical men for rule. That may have been obscure to the reformers themselves, but it influenced them nevertheless, and it was to be the paramount issue in the future of the Reformation all over Europe.

ACQUISITIVE BURGHERS, *a moneylender and his wife weigh their receipts in a portrait ordered to proclaim their success.*

THE NEW MONEYED CLASS

While the Reformation was reshaping Europe's religious mores, an economic revolution was changing the daily lives of Protestants and Catholics alike. Under the pressure of expanding trade, the old concepts of barter and land-based wealth gave way to a money economy whose sovereign principle was that capital could and should be used to create more capital. The new materialism was slyly satirized by artist Quentin Massys in the painting above: he showed the moneylender's work distracting his wife's attention from her Bible. Many such merchants won fame, power and even titles. And in their pursuit of profit, they nourished a great boom by developing many business institutions and practices in use today— including stock exchanges, letters of credit, bills of transfer and bank deposits.

SILVER COINS *depict the men who minted them. They are, from top, double thalers of Frederick of Saxony, and Albert, Archbishop of Mainz; a half-thaler of Count Jacob Fugger; and a thaler of Emperor Charles V.*

The Mixed Blessings of Modern Finance

The 16th Century business boom brought prosperity to many—and problems to all. As the English statesman Thomas More declared, gold and silver had become "the blood of the whole body social," and trade expanded under huge transfusions of the precious stuff. The supply of metals available for coinage doubled and redoubled as improved mining methods increased the yield of European mines, and as ships returned laden with gold and silver from Africa, the Orient and the New World.

But this vast treasure entered the arteries of commerce through a bewildering variety of mints. Kingdoms large and small coined money; so did free cities, and duchies ruled by noblemen and clerics. Moreover, these authorities compounded the difficulties of dealing in so many currencies by periodically reducing the content of precious metal in their alloys—a practice that helped force prices up and up. During the century, the cost of a bushel of wheat rose as much as 200 per cent in France, 300 per cent in Germany. People everywhere were caught in the grip of a powerful trend whose name, coined later, has become all too familiar: inflation.

MONEYMAKERS *coin silver thalers in the German town of Annaberg. A blank metal disk, heated red hot, was placed on a die by a man with tongs; a co-worker covers the disk with another die and strikes it with an iron mallet.*

Here on this side we discuss
things of secrecy and importance
which concern mining operations;
thus the Merchant's Company will profit.

I am called the Secret Book.
My master doesn't entrust me to anyone
because he keeps his dealings to himself.

THE BOOK OF SECRETS

INVENTORY BOOK

By land I travel here with letters,
what they say I do not know;
I make my masters happy with them,
but also grumpy and anxious.

JUDG MENT OR CHOICE

Being sensible and quite careful
brings big returns.

In the journal, I write every day
with accuracy and skill
all that occurs in the Company.
That surely makes for good reporting.

The Company requires people who
are upright in word and deed and—
this you mark well— whose hearts
and tongues are in agreement.

INTEGRITY

He who administers
much should keep i
As I must do many
I carefully keep the

The treasury I do administer—
receipts and outlays, actually.
The till I do often check,
and what's left over I carry carefully.

KNOWLEDGE OF LANGUAGES

I have a knowledge of languages
and therefore the Company needs me too.
Using these, I buy and sell goods properly,
and without loss or danger.

Lady Luck is showing here the sphere
on which the riches of the world rest.
All things, soon shattered,
meet here with death their end.
Therefore note the wind-blown smoke,
be pious, fearing God, and do penance.

*The office established here manages
the common treasury.
All the small and petty payments
are duly taken care of here.*

*From the journal into the ledger,
and also into the master ledger, I enter
debits on the left-hand side;
on the right-hand side belong the credits.*

*This is called the counting table.
Nimbly counted on it is the money
with which the bills are paid;
one has to make good on them to others.*

SILENCE

*He who would be lucky in the Company
doesn't borrow much outside money,
and he doesn't let the increase grow for long
because it would discomfort him.
From bad debts he should
carefully protect himself in advance.*

*He who would trade in the merchant's way,
but doesn't know his profits or his losses,
nor even how he stands with everyone,
and what he should be collecting
(the same thing also with his payments)—
he indeed should keep in mind
not to write on playing cards,
but to stick to his ledgers
and diligently enter all his dealings;
his business otherwise will not be lasting.*

Bands of Merchants
in Quest of Profit

To increase their efficiency—and profits—merchants and bankers pooled their resources and formed companies that were prototypes of today's business corporations. One such firm, imaginary but typical, is depicted in this allegorical print, made in 1585. The firm's many specialists —bookkeepers, cashiers, couriers, middlemen who were skilled linguists—describe their jobs in quaint verses, translated here from the original German. At top center, the head of the company is seated beneath the firm's master ledger, which he alone could consult. At bottom center stands Lady Luck, a popularized version of the Goddess of Fortune, who was believed to determine the fate of all man's ventures.

The operations of a great commercial house were far-flung, diversified and complex. Most firms depended for the bulk of their income on interest from loans and on profits obtained from fluctuations in prices and exchange rates. In addition, many firms invested heavily in mining, industry and real estate. By these various enterprises, a few houses grew so powerful that kings came to them to finance wars.

GAMBLING AT CARDS, *four burghers, each one advised by a kibitzer, puzzle over the play of a hand. The cards they are using have plain white backs—a deterrent to cheaters who were skilled at marking fancy-backed decks.*

SELLING INDULGENCES *under symbols of papal authority, clerics and bankers' agents collect money from Catholic townspeople for form letters absolving sins. The sale price varied according to the buyer's social class.*

"When Did Avarice Reign More Largely?"

Inevitably, the new money economy fostered many deplorable practices. The prospects of easy gain excited ruinous speculation, lotteries and other forms of gambling. Catholics were exploited by the sale of indulgences, which exempted sinners from penalties for a price—and gave rake-offs to the bankers who handled these revenues for the Church. Though lending money for profit was officially banned by the Church and carefully policed by Protestant sects, annual interest rates often rose to 22 per cent on small loans. As in every age, outcries against corruption were raised, and the scholar Erasmus of Rotterdam railed in anguish, "When did avarice reign more largely and less punished?"

COLLECTING TAXES, *an agent eagerly seizes a lady's payment. Because taxes were hard to collect, kings had to rely on loans from bankers.*

A Businessman Who Scolded a King

To 16th Century men, Jacob Fugger of Augsburg was living proof that every height could be scaled by an ambitious commoner with a head for business. Fugger, the grandson of a weaver, and the son of a successful merchant, parlayed his inheritance into a financial empire that included banks, mines, factories and farm lands. Earning an average annual profit of 54 per cent for 16 years, he became the richest man in Europe; he crowned his success by acquiring a castle and the title of count.

Held in awe by the pope and Luther alike, Fugger was so sure of his power that in 1523 he dared to write a dunning letter to his perennial debtor, Charles V of the Holy Roman Empire. Reminding Charles that "Your Majesty could not have secured the Roman Crown without me," Fugger bluntly—and successfully—advised the Emperor to make payment on a loan, "without any further delay."

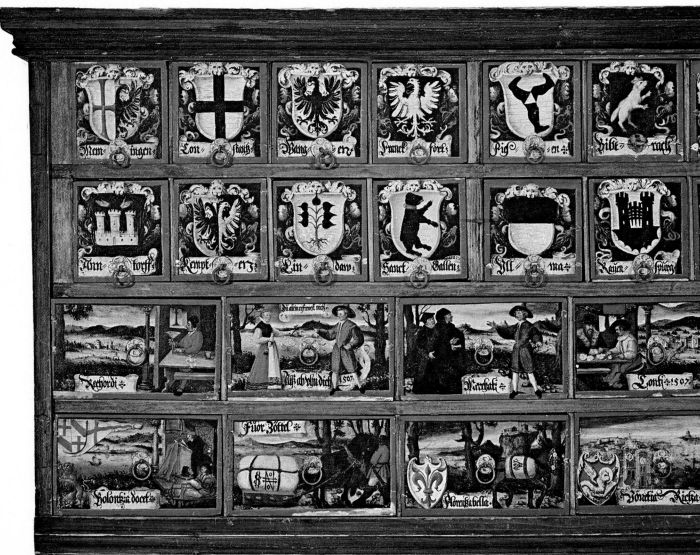

A MORTGAGE *on a count's castle bears the* Fugger *seal, cut to show the loan was repaid.*

A GREAT FINANCIER, *Jacob Fugger (right) is seen with his trusted book-keeper Matthaus Schwartz in a painting done by Schwartz himself in 1516. The cabinet at rear bears the names of cities in which Fugger's branch of-fices were located. Among them were Rome, Budapest, Cracow and Lisbon.*

A DECORATED CHEST *was used to file letters in Fugger's Augsburg office. Upper drawers display crests of duchies and cities in which Fugger did business; below are scenes from everyday life. In the third row, second drawer from left, a young man tells a woman, "You delight me."*

The Antwerp Bourse, a Crossroads of Trade

The greatest center of 16th Century commerce—a combination stock exchange and marketplace—was the Bourse at Antwerp, seen here in a contemporary engraving. At lower left appears the Bourse's motto, dated 1531 and posted above a doorway to the quadrangle: "For the service of merchants of all nations and languages."

To this clearinghouse each week came fabulous merchandise from near and far, delivered by thousands of ships and wagons. Each day, amid the hubbub of colorful crowds, everything useful or valuable was put on sale: Spanish lace and Venetian glass; tin from England and spices from the Orient; the services of professional soldiers and assassins; and, in a gallery on the second floor, paintings by great Flemish artists. In the rush to buy, petty tradesmen and naïve investors rubbed elbows with lordly wholesalers and cynical speculators. "All of these persons," wrote a noted Italian visitor, "being people who are earning money, invest it not only in commerce but also in building, in buying lands and properties . . . and thus from day to day the city keeps on growing, and flourishes, and increases marvellously."

S. P. Q. A.
IN VSVM NEGOTIATORVM
CVIVSCVMQ. NATIONIS AC LINGVÆ
VRBISQ. ADEO SVÆ ORNAMENTVM
ANNO M. D. XXXI.
A SOLO EXTRVI CVR.

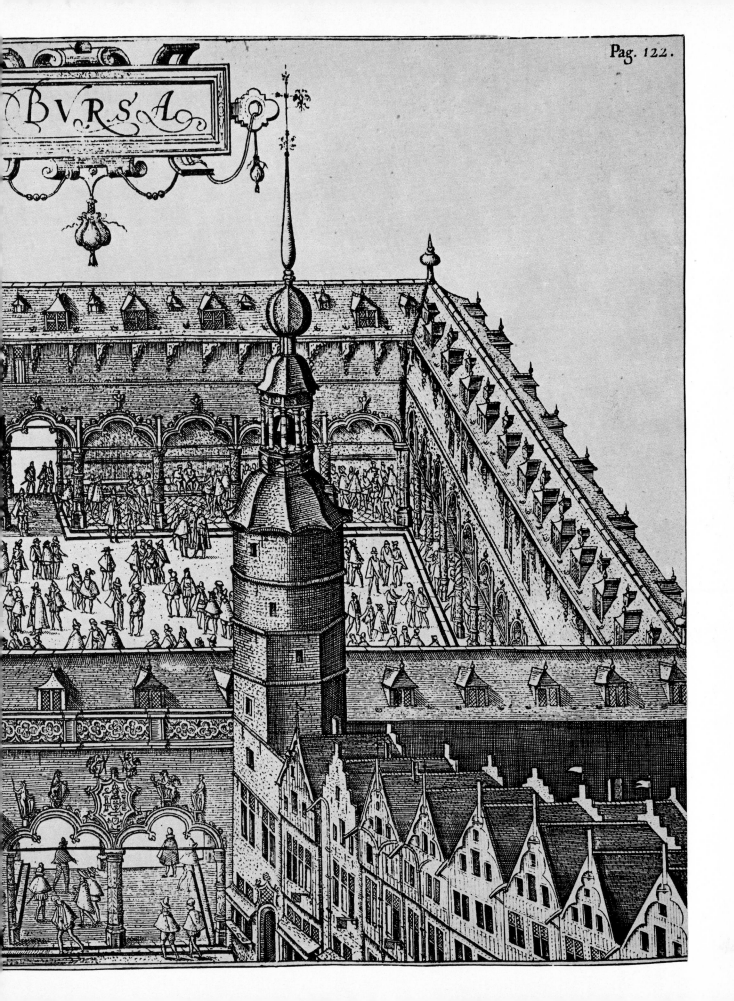

BVRSA

4

EUROPE AROUSED

Revolutions seldom bring about the visionary's dream; they are metamorphosed by other men with other dreams. So it was with the Reformation. The movement that Luther, Zwingli, Calvin and Knox launched in the desire to lead men to personal salvation became in the end a political phenomenon.

From the beginning the impulse to reform the Church had mingled with political currents. But the spiritual impulse was dominated by dynastic intrigue, greed and war, and in the end national politics determined the fate of the Reformation all over Europe. What began in a mood of spiritual piety had its triumph in a rearrangement of secular power. In this respect the Reformation marks the beginning of modern times—of the ascendancy of the state over religion.

When the Edict of Worms was issued in 1521 Catholicism seemed invincible. The Emperor Charles was sworn to stamp out heresy. The obstinate Luther was outlawed, and the preaching of his ideas was made an offense against the Empire.

Then the support that Luther had once had appeared to wane. Before the year was out, the urbane and erudite Erasmus broke with him, and other scholars followed suit. Their wish from the beginning had been to reform the Church, not destroy it, and to raise the intellectual standards of the Christian world. Not only was Luther rupturing the institution; in the eyes of some he was erecting the foundations for another tyranny in its place. The loss of the intellectuals meant the addition of a strong force against him, for the men of that class who deserted Luther returned to the support of the Church.

Greater even than this loss, in terms of numbers, at least, was the disenchantment of the lower classes. The peasants, excited by Luther's denunciation of authority, had taken him at his word and rebelled against the lords. When he wrote a stinging tract reprimanding the peasants and urging the authorities to take action against them, he alienated the lower classes.

Nevertheless, the Lutheran cause retained great strength. Its main appeal was to the princes, the nobility and the burghers—people who were sufficiently powerful to thwart political interference from Rome; sufficiently prosperous to resent the economic drain of taxation by the papacy; sufficiently educated to discard medieval superstitions; sufficiently self-confident to balk at having their consciences dictated to.

The Emperor's oath to defend the faith did nothing to dissuade these groups from their Lutheran inclinations. The princes were historically opposed to imperial authority. The burghers, like burghers in every country of Europe, were developing a national consciousness; and Charles, who had been reared in the Netherlands and never learned to speak proper German, was regarded as a foreigner. Luther's call to established authority endeared him to the princes, and his attack on the drain of money to Italy struck a vital chord among the money-making townsmen. One by one princes were won over to Luther's religion, and one by one cities followed. A few remained loyal to the Catholic faith and to the Emperor; the result was the growth of two political factions: one Catholic and the other Lutheran.

But the real advantage to the Lutheran cause lay in the Emperor's preoccupation with international politics. Charles's far-flung domains made him look formidable in the 16th Century, but the very extent of these territories was a drawback. In allowing his eye to be diverted abroad, Charles neglected what was happening in Germany. He warred with France, which for years had been antipathetic to the Habsburgs; with the Turks, who were encroaching on Hungary; and even with his sometime ally, the pope. Not until 1529, eight years after the Edict of Worms, did he turn his attention to Germany. When he did, it was only to send word to a Diet that was meeting at Speyer, an imperial city in the Rhineland Palatinate, that the Edict of Worms was to be enforced and Catholic worship restored.

He was too late. By that time many of the princes and cities had already taken over local regulation of the Church and instituted Lutheran practices. Several princes and 14 cities drew up a solemn protest against Charles's order. They came to be known as the "Protesting Estates," and subsequently the name "Protestants" was given to all who left the Roman Church.

This protest at last aroused Charles to address himself in earnest to the religious question. He came to Germany in 1530 and called a Diet at Augsburg to which he summoned leading theologians of both persuasions—but not Luther, who was still outlawed.

Both sides met in a spirit of conciliation. The Protestants, making what was to be their last effort to have their ideas accepted by the Church, endeavored to prove that there was in Lutheran thought "nothing repugnant to Scripture or to the Roman Church." They presented a general statement of their beliefs, the cardinal point of which was that justification of the soul should be by faith alone. (This statement, which is known as the Confession of Augsburg, remains to this day as the creed of the Lutheran Church, and it has influenced the drawing up of subsequent creeds.)

The theologians tried to debate, but they could not come to agreement. The Emperor dismissed the Diet, promising to urge the pope to call an ecumenical council to decide on the points in dispute. The Lutherans were ordered in the meantime to return to Catholic practices by April 15, 1531.

Charles succeeded only in intensifying the antagonism of the Protestants. Faced with the threat of coercion, six princes and representatives of 10 cities convened in February at Schmalkalden, a little town in central Germany, and formed a military alliance known as the Schmalkaldic League. Other princes and towns sought admission to the league, and within 15 years it had grown to include most of the Protestant Estates of the Empire. It fortified the position of Protestantism and established the Protestant party as a strong political force in Germany.

A VICTORIOUS EMPEROR, *Charles V stands over Francis I of France on an elaborately carved "handstone." Towns offered such objects to visiting monarchs as flattering bribes to protect their property—and women—from the royal guard.*

Over a period of more than 20 years Charles made sporadic attempts at negotiation with the Protestants, but he was still distracted by events outside Germany—further war with France, incursions by the Turks into Austria and Hungary, and efforts to secure the Crown of the Empire for his brother Ferdinand. When Charles finally called his last Diet, in 1555, the Lutherans had grown to such numbers that they demanded and received recognition. The result was the Peace of Augsburg, a treaty providing that every prince and every free city should have the right to decide whether the people under his or its jurisdiction should be Catholic or Lutheran.

This was not a treaty signaling toleration in the modern sense. It provided only for Lutherans and Catholics, and not at all for Anabaptists and Calvinists, who now had some adherents in the Empire. Anyone disagreeing with the faith of the prince or the city administration had the option of moving elsewhere, but he did not have the freedom to remain and worship as he chose. The historical importance of the treaty lay in the fact that it conceded the existence of two religious points of view, and in this it was even more remarkable than the historic Diet of Worms. Worms had foreshadowed the end of medieval unity; Augsburg made this a fact. At Worms a single man had spoken his mind in defiance of the established order, but he had been outlawed; at Augsburg the principles he voiced gained legal sanction.

From a religious point of view, Augsburg was a victory; from a national point of view, it was a defeat, for in strengthening the rights of the princes it frustrated political unity. While other nations solidified as mighty powers, the German people were to remain divided and weak for another 300 years.

Though it went counter to the trend toward national unity that was prevailing elsewhere in Europe, the Peace of Augsburg was nevertheless consistent with another trend that was equally prevalent: the move toward secular determination of religious affairs. By 1555, when the Peace of Augsburg gave the territorial states in Germany the right to opt for either of two religions, England had already forged a state religion of its own.

Luther's theses had been sent by Erasmus to a colleague in London shortly after their publication in 1517. After this, Lutheran ideas slipped in gradually—largely through England's trade with the Netherlands, Germany's neighbor and cultural cousin. If the result was doctrinal variation from Catholicism, however, little attention was paid it by the people at large, for the English were less inflammable over matters of dogma than the Germans.

But there were other movements afoot, and a process was set in motion that was the reverse of Germany's. Whereas in Germany the princes and burghers adopted the new faith first and the Emperor was obliged to give it recognition, in England the monarchs saw state advantages to Church reform and the people followed them. The process began in the 1520s, the same decade in which Luther was outlawed in Germany. It began with King Henry VIII.

Henry was a singularly popular and effective King: he was handsome, athletic, learned and generous to his favorites. He was also egotistical, despotic and perfidious. By his actions in domestic and foreign affairs he wrought the most sweeping social changes of the 16th Century—but they were changes that came so gradually and so legally that their full effect would not be realized until the reign of his daughter Elizabeth.

When he came to the throne in 1509, Henry married Catherine of Aragon, who was the widow of his brother Arthur. She was the daughter of Ferdinand and Isabella of Spain (and hence she was also the aunt of the Emperor Charles V). The marriage was made for purely political motives—to reinforce an alliance with Spain against France. Spain soon formed another alliance with France, thus making itself less attractive to Henry than formerly. But more important, Catherine failed in the most important duty incumbent on a queen: she gave Henry no son to inherit the throne. Only one of her children survived, and that was Mary, a pale, thin and introspective girl. It was not at all certain at the time that a woman could legally inherit the throne of England.

Henry's marriage to Catherine had been questioned at the beginning; he had needed a papal dispensation to marry his sister-in-law—a dispensation that the pope granted as a favor to Ferdinand and Isabella. When there was no male heir after more than a decade, people recalled the words of the Book of Leviticus, that "if a man shall take his brother's wife . . . they shall be childless." This was a religious and a superstitious age, and the heirless Henry, no less than his simplest subject, wondered if he were being punished by God.

Meanwhile, he had become infatuated with Anne Boleyn, a dark-haired lady-in-waiting to Queen Catherine. Anne was no beauty, but she possessed enough power in her slender person to demand a price for her favors to Henry—and she wanted to be Queen.

Probably in hopes of begetting a male heir (for Anne was now pregnant), perhaps only because he was tired of Catherine (who had grown withered and unattractive), Henry decided to marry Anne Boleyn. He ordered Thomas Cardinal Wolsey—who held both civil and religious offices as Archbishop of York, Chancellor of the Realm, and Papal Legate to England—to secure a papal annulment of his marriage to Catherine.

Wolsey was a gifted statesman, but most Englishmen despised him. He was the new-rich son of a butcher, and had risen to eminence by currying royal favor. He was vain, self-seeking, and given to extravagant displays of his wealth and power. He taxed the people heavily. He had an ambitious foreign policy that threatened war with the Emperor Charles V, whose Netherlands were the best customers of the English merchants. He boasted of his link with Rome and explained many of his unpopular acts by claiming to speak in the name of the Pope, thus intensifying in clergy and laymen alike an already existing aversion to the Holy See. This was the man Henry dispatched to secure an annulment of his marriage.

Annulments were not uncommon in this era; monarchs might receive them as political favors from popes. But in this instance Pope Clement VII had other political considerations besides Henry. Charles V was loath to sever the tenuous link he had with England through his aunt. His armies stood in Italy, threatening violence if the Pope consented to the divorce of Charles's aunt. Clement, a weak and ineffectual man, was unnerved by the dilemma he faced. Wishing not to alienate either ruler, he wrung his hands and procrastinated. Wolsey's usual diplomatic finesse failed him; he delivered no annulment. Henry therefore dismissed the Cardinal from office in 1529 and took up the matter himself.

Henry now proceeded, by a series of cautious, legal steps, to sever his nation from Rome. First he married Anne Boleyn in secret. Next he appointed a new Archbishop of Canterbury, Thomas Cranmer, whom he instructed to declare his marriage to Catherine void on the grounds that it had been illegal to begin with. Cranmer obliged and Anne was crowned Queen of England. Then, to rationalize his actions, Henry persuaded Parliament to pass the Act in Restraint of Appeals, denying all jurisdiction of foreign powers in English affairs—implicitly meaning the jurisdiction of Rome in royal marriage. Pope Clement VII, finally aroused, struck back

by excommunicating Henry and declaring his marriage to Anne invalid. National feeling was strong, however, and the people supported the King.

And Henry had only begun. By the Act of Supremacy he had Parliament name him supreme head of the Church in England—a title Parliament readily gave, for Wolsey had crystallized English resentment against the Church of Rome. By other parliamentary acts Henry assumed the right to make all ecclesiastical appointments, and he required all clergymen to swear allegiance to himself instead of the Pope.

Finally, by the Act of Dissolution, he dissolved most of the monasteries. He confiscated their land and their wealth, which he lavishly tossed to the eager gentry. The monks were given the option of joining the few monasteries that were allowed to remain, or of entering the secular clergy.

Henry had no Lutherlike quarrel with dogma; he wanted power, and he got it by presenting his case to a willing people like an affronted monarch resisting a foreign tyrant in the person of the Pope. Only two men of note refused to comply with Henry's demand for allegiance. One was John Fisher, Bishop of Rochester, a kindly and elderly humanist who was Catherine's confessor and her chief defender. The other was Sir Thomas More, the first nonecclesiastic to hold the post of Chancellor in England, and a brilliant author. With his book *Utopia* (a coinage from the Greek meaning "no place") he gave a word to the English language and a concept to Western literature. *Utopia* was a tale told by a traveler returned from a strange new world where men were uncorrupted by vice, where reason and beauty and law worked in harmony to make the perfect society.

Both More and Fisher saw tragedy in the sundering of Christendom, and they perceived tyranny in Henry's acts at a time when others were too inflated by national self-consciousness to controvert

HENRY VIII EDWARD VI MARY I

the royal rationalizations. Because they refused to obey the King, More and Fisher were beheaded for treason. But these were atypical acts of bloodshed in an otherwise orderly revolution.

Only three years after his marriage, Henry tired of Anne. Her offense was probably the same as Catherine's, that she produced no male heir (she had only a daughter, Elizabeth), but Henry accused her of adultery and incest, and sent her to the Tower of London and then to the execution block. He took another wife, Jane Seymour, who had the good fortune to produce a son—Edward, a frail and sickly child but a bright one, and a male heir.

Henry's culminating move came in 1536, when he directed the drawing up of a definition of faith and the Book of Common Prayer. This was no move prompted by religious piety; it was done in the interest of precluding schism in the King's domain. The definition was drawn up at Henry's behest by clergymen who conferred at first with theologians at Wittenberg. Henry, however, had considerable knowledge of theology himself, and he rejected the Wittenberg-inspired definition as too unorthodox. Several other definitions followed, until finally, with the publication of the "King's Book" in 1543, Henry arrived at a creed that was thoroughly Catholic except for its emphasis on the authority of the Bible and on justification by faith. Its

significance, however, was in its issuance by the government. Hearing of it in Germany, Luther said: "This King wants to be God. He founds articles of faith, which even the Pope never did." Later, when Henry declared Romanists traitors and Lutherans heretics, Luther thanked God that he and his followers were rid of the blasphemer who had tried to enter their fold.

When Henry died in 1547 (having married three more childless wives), Edward was a boy of nine, and two regents governed in turn. Edward died at 15, and the incumbent regent, the Earl of Northumberland, endeavored to seat his own family on the throne. But the English people had learned to love the monarchy, and they wanted a royal heir. Pushing aside their prejudice against women, they turned enthusiastically to Henry's elder daughter, Mary. She was dour and ailing, but she had suffered outrages and neglect, and this gave her a certain appeal.

Mary's appeal did not last long. Her sufferings had embittered her without teaching her understanding. Disregarding national sentiment against Spain, she married her cousin, King Philip II. Failing to perceive how little the people cared for dogma, or how strong was their aversion to Rome as a foreign power, she supposed that her own sudden popularity represented enthusiasm for the faith of her disgraced mother. Clinging steadfastly to that faith, she tried to restore its practices in England.

CHARLES V

WILLIAM OF ORANGE

REFORMATION DYNASTIES *reflected the religious disputes of the times. England's Henry VIII (far left) broke with Rome to gain a male heir; ironically, the death of his son Edward VI brought a Catholic to the throne —Henry's daughter Mary. In Holland, William of Orange, once a page to the Habsburg Emperor Charles V, led Protestant rebels to victory against Charles's pious Catholic son.*

She began moderately, but her attitude grew more intolerant and her methods harsher. She annulled the acts passed in Henry's and Edward's reigns and replaced them with others persecuting heresy.

Mary's persecution served only to make the people want Protestantism the more—not for its dogma, but because it seemed to represent freedom from tyranny. Like her celebrated cousin and father-in-law, Emperor Charles V, Mary died a failure. Both suffered the same tragic flaw. They had strong convictions of faith, but they could not grasp the significance of their subjects' sentiments.

When Mary died in 1558, Englishmen joyfully acclaimed Elizabeth, because she seemed to promise peace. Elizabeth proved to be a masterly ruler, in character and in politics the very opposite of her half-sister. Having no strong faith herself, she took care to offend none of her subjects; and knowing the value of mental privacy she said she would make "no windows into men's souls."

Unlike Mary, Elizabeth had from childhood been wooed to her father's ideas. She was 17 years Mary's junior—too young to suffer vicariously her mother's disgrace, young enough to be inculcated with the same ideas that made her father popular. Also, she was by nature pragmatic, which Mary was not. She was swayed by the knowledge that, although a great many people in England remained Catholic, the influential classes were Protestant. In England,

as in Germany, Protestantism appealed to the landed gentry and the aggressive burghers, and Elizabeth needed the support of these to rule. She reigned for 45 years, and in that time she brought her island country from provincial insularity to international importance.

Under her reign Parliament repealed the legislation of Mary's reign, seized the little land that remained to the Church of Rome, drew up another definition of faith and revised the Book of Common Prayer. The articles of faith determined in her reign are still fundamental to the Anglican creed.

The Church that evolved under Elizabeth was a compromise. It took matters of dogma, such as justification by faith and the nature of the sacraments, primarily from Luther (though enough ambiguity remained to satisfy widely different beliefs and to allow for privacy of conscience). It retained the ritual and erected a hierarchy modeled on the Church of Rome—the difference being that the monarch, instead of the pope, was the head.

The course that England took represents the triumph of the monarchy over the Church; that of the Netherlands represents the beginnings of modern republicanism. In the Netherlands perhaps more than in any other country religion took effect on burgher mentality and intertwined with political circumstances to alter both church and state.

The Netherlands in the 16th Century included approximately the same territory that today constitutes Belgium, Holland and Luxembourg, plus a strip of northern France. The territory was a crossroads of Germanic and Latin culture and language. Germanic influences predominated in the north and Latin in the south. As Habsburg property it was under the suzerainty of the Emperor Charles V, who was himself a Netherlander. It came under the political domination of Spain in 1555, when Charles bequeathed it to his son Philip along with the Crown of Spain.

By a privilege dating back a century, when the territory was ruled by the Duke of Burgundy (Charles V's great-grandfather), the people were partly self-governing, having an Estates-General, or assembly of nobles and bourgeoisie, modeled on that of France. They had been virtually autonomous since 1530 because Charles, as King of Spain and Emperor, left them much to themselves.

The people of this area were sturdy and self-reliant, hardened by centuries of stemming the sea and reclaiming the land. Geographic and natural elements also made the country rich and an entrepôt of ideas. The Rhine, the Scheldt, the Meuse and dozens of other waterways crisscrossed the country, carrying the commerce of interior Europe inland from the coast, where great natural ports harbored the fleets of Spain and Portugal, England and Italy. Antwerp alone in the 16th Century had 2,500 ships anchored at a time, and of these as many as 500 sailed in a day. (This is approximately the same number of planes that flew out of New York International Airport on an average day in 1965.) Not only in Antwerp, but in Rotterdam, Amsterdam, Utrecht and Leyden, merchants congregated with cargoes of wool, gold and spices, and exchanged ideas with zeal and curiosity.

As a clearinghouse of ideas, the Netherlands bred intellectuals. Their lower schools were unsurpassed and their illustrious scholars (of whom the cosmopolitan Erasmus was only one) were renowned all over Europe. They had scores of printing presses (50 new publishers sprang up in the years between 1525 and 1555) and there was a high rate of literacy among nobles and bourgeoisie alike.

Inevitably, the scholars and merchants brought in the new religious ideas—Lutheranism, Anabaptism and Calvinism. Of all these, the one that was to implant itself most indelibly on the national character was Calvinism. Its strongest appeal was to those who had grown rich by self-assertion and were therefore ready to quarrel with the established power, but in time it won much of the aristocracy, too. Its emphasis on frugality, hard work and self-reliance won ready acceptance among a people who had cultivated these very qualities in fighting the sea and reclaiming the land. Its doctrine of the elect gave them moral support under persecution. Its disciplined organization provided a framework that was politically useful in a land where the monarch was absent.

The Netherlanders had had a profound affection for the Emperor Charles V; even his edicts against heresy—which he promulgated here as in Germany —failed to alienate them, for they regarded Charles as one of themselves and, as far as they were able, they simply neglected to enforce the edicts. They accepted his son, Philip II, cheerfully enough on his accession, but they soon learned to despise him. Philip, a melancholy man who sincerely believed himself chosen by God to play a historic role, was a conscientious ruler who spent long hours reading dispatches and planning public works. He believed that the monarchy was absolute and that the Church, its ally, was essential to social order. Though he had the blond complexion of his northern forebears, he was thoroughly Spanish in upbringing and temperament, and he never learned to understand the Netherlanders' character.

Spanish and Netherlandish ideals were poles apart. The Spaniard prized wealth, but wealth to him meant land. He was unaccustomed to banking and trade, and he looked with disdain on the newfangled preoccupation with commerce. So Philip arrived at a policy in keeping with both Spanish sentiment and Dutch resources; he taxed the commerce that he held in contempt. In addition, he appointed his own officials to both secular and ecclesiastical posts, depriving the Netherlanders of administrative and judicial rights they had been developing for more than 100 years. Finally, he installed an army of Spanish troops.

If the Netherlanders' commercial enterprise was distasteful to the Spanish, their unorthodoxy was abhorrent. Philip said he would die 100 deaths rather than be king of heretics. It seemed Spain's historic destiny to fight the heathen. For hundreds of years Catholic Spain had waged ferocious war against the Moslem infidel, and the effect of the prolonged conflict had been to impregnate the Spanish soul with mixed strains of brooding mysticism, rigid orthodoxy and angry intolerance. In the 16th Century the Netherlands beckoned Spain to a new crusade on which Philip embarked with terrible zeal. To eradicate their heresies he imposed the Inquisition, an institution that had been inaugurated in Spain nearly 100 years before by his great-grandparents, Ferdinand and Isabella, for use against the Jews and Moslems.

Ill feeling over all these grievances simmered for a decade. Finally it found expression among a group of powerful nobles who in 1566 presented to Philip's regent a petition calling for abolition of the Inquisition and for the summoning of an Estates-General to deal with the religious question. One of the regent's coterie said contemptuously, *"Ce n'est qu'un tas de gueux"*—"They're nothing but a mass of beggars." The nobles and their followers adopted the title for themselves. Henceforth they were the *Gueux*, the Beggars, and the beggar's money belt and food bowl became the symbol of their revolt.

Behind these noble Beggars stood several powerful figures, among them Lamoral, Count of Egmont, and William, Prince of Orange. Egmont, who was brilliant and valorous in war, radiated a charm that captivated his contemporaries and future generations alike; two centuries after his time the legends that survived about him were to inspire Goethe to drama and Beethoven to music. Orange, an educated man who spoke seven languages, was called William the Silent for his penchant for keeping his own counsel. He was born the richest man in the Netherlands; he left his children almost penniless, having sold most of his possessions to raise money for the cause of his countrymen.

Neither Egmont nor Orange was ardently religious; both were prompted by the desire to end Spanish oppression, and in this they represented popular sentiment. They were members of the regent's council, and despite Philip's reign of terror they were loyal to the principle of monarchy, for they wanted independence without rebellion.

But the same popular sentiment that these nobles represented was being fanned by other men less conservative than they. Calvinist missionaries had by this time dispersed from Switzerland and France, and were heatedly preaching against the evils of tyranny. In August 1566, not long after the nobles had presented their petition to the regent, riots broke out in Armentières, then spread to Antwerp, Brussels, Ghent, and north to the provinces of Holland and Zeeland. Like the uprising of the American Colonies in 1775, this rebellion had at its roots the rising resentment of an adolescent nation against absentee rule and extortionate taxation. In the case of the Netherlands the resentment was compounded by religious persecution, and it was therefore in religion that it made itself manifest. Mobs broke into churches, hammered the statuary to shards, shattered stained-glass windows and burned Catholic books. Egmont and Orange at first tried to quell the disturbances, but riot erupted into war.

To crush the rebels Philip dispatched Fernando Alvarez de Toledo, Duke of Alva, a terrible figure of merciless discipline and sanctimonious piety. Alva had inherited a vast estate at the age of 20; now, at 59, he had for several years been serving Philip on the battlefield and in the council of state, exhibiting valor and severity in both. He looked the very model of an El Greco painting: tall and thin, with dark, somber eyes and a beard the color of Toledo steel.

In 1567 Alva marched 10,000 soldiers into the Netherlands, where he inaugurated a ruthless dictatorship and a long and savage war that was to decimate the population, despoil the land and cripple the prosperity that had flourished for hundreds of years. He established a Council of Troubles, a tribunal designed to deal with rebellion as the Inquisition dealt with heresy, and it soon became popularly known as the Council of Blood. Thousands of people implicated in treason were done to death, among them Egmont, who was publicly beheaded. Orange, escaping Alva's apprehension, fled to Germany, where he raised an army of 25,000 men. He returned to organize all the provinces of the Netherlands in opposition to Philip. Many of the people were still Catholic in faith, but the issue now was foreign tyranny, not religion.

The south, which was under more Latin influence and weaker economically, was conquered by Spain and remained with the Church. As a political territory it was tossed hither and yon for another three centuries, passing subsequently under the domination of Austria, France and the Netherlands, until finally it emerged in the 19th Century as the nations of Belgium and Luxembourg.

But the north controlled the sea and was better able to withstand the war. In 1581 seven northern provinces declared their independence from Spain and established a new government—a government that was now predominantly Calvinist in religion, but that allowed for varying worship. Orange served as its chief for the next three years, until he was shot in his own house by a Catholic fanatic after Philip had offered a reward for his head. Bloodshed continued for years, but the people for whom William of Orange had given his wealth and his life held out. Eventually they formed the Dutch Republic, which in the 17th Century was to recover the wealth lost during 50 years of extortion and war and to become the leader of all Europe in finance, art and colonization of foreign lands. This tiny nation, no bigger than the state of Maryland, was to spread to the rest of the Western world a spirit of temperance and industry—and, eventually, tolerance.

By the time that the Dutch rebellion began, half a century had passed since the publication of Luther's Theses, and Protestantism in one form or another had penetrated all over Europe. The ideas generated by the Reformation were to remain fundamental to Western thought, but as a movement the Reformation now began to run down. It met its first significant defeat in France.

In France, as elsewhere, there had been early preaching for reform, but in France the reforming spirit was primarily Christian humanism—an attempt among intellectual Catholics to cross the strains of classical ethics with the piety of the people. And humanism never did take root among the people at large; it was too intellectual, too abstract.

All over Europe the interplay between people and rulers had determined the fate of the Reformation, and France was no exception. In that century, no significant numbers of people wanted the Reformation, and the state did not need it. In 1516, by the Concordat of Bologna, a treaty made by King Francis I with the papacy, the French King was granted the right to make ecclesiastical nominations—the same right that Henry VIII secured from Parliament without consulting the pope. Because he used ecclesiastical appointments as patronage to reward officials and courtiers for their services, and because he took substantial revenue in Church taxes, the French King would have gained no advantage by upsetting the status quo.

Francis I was an extravagant man and an opportunist. He was not a militant Catholic by any means, nor were the members of his family. His sister, Margaret of Angoulême, was attracted to the new doctrines; she gave haven to the persecuted and was herself the author of *The Mirror of the Sinful Soul*, a pious tract of questionable orthodoxy. King Francis shifted his political alliances among the pope, the German princes, and even the Turks, as it suited his purposes. When he wanted to court the favor of the pope or the French clergy, he engaged in intermittent persecution; when he sought the support of the German princes in opposition to Charles V, he let the Protestants alone. His son, Henry II, engaged in somewhat harsher persecution in an otherwise uneventful reign.

When Henry II died in 1559, he left his wife, Catherine de' Medici (daughter of the famous Italian banking family and a niece of Pope Clement VII) and a frail brood of heirs, the eldest of whom was 15. One after another three kings came to the throne, and one after another they died. Catherine ruled all of them. She was a shrewd woman who had no scruples about playing on the vanities of her subjects for political ends. Her aim was national peace, but her hand was unsteady and the monarchy therefore weakened.

Its weakness allowed the rise of several dissident political factions; and in France, as elsewhere, political antagonism was asserted in religious terms. In the first of these factions were the ardent Catholics, who stood for orthodoxy, for the extirpation of heresy, and, generally but not always, for support of the Crown. Their champion was the Duke of Guise, leader of the French military forces and head of a family whom the favors of Henry II had raised to national prominence.

The other group comprised the Protestants, called Huguenots for reasons that are now unclear. They were disciples of Calvin, and the more visionary among them wanted to make the French nation over in the austere pattern of Calvin's theocracy in Geneva. They were few in numbers but strong in organization. Most of their members, like the members of Protestant groups everywhere, came from the commercial class, but they had a few important adherents among the nobility.

The Catholic and Huguenot factions struggled intermittently against each other, and for and against the Crown. Catherine, who had no particular religious convictions of her own, knew that the overwhelming majority of her people were Catholic. But she also knew that the Huguenots could keep the state in constant turmoil if they were not given consideration. To keep the peace she passed a series of edicts, the last of which granted the Huguenots limited freedom of worship. Nobles were allowed to hold services in their own domains, and certain towns were allowed Protestant chapels. The people chafed under the restrictions, but they had in fact considerable freedom for a minority group in the early 1560s.

In a further move to win the good will of the Huguenots, Catherine arranged the marriage of her daughter Margaret to Henry of Navarre, who was the titular leader of the Huguenot party. He was also, as the grandson of Margaret of Angoulême, Francis I's sister, next in line to the throne after Catherine's children.

But the marriage that was to have brought peace brought instead one of the bloodiest disasters of a bloody age: the Massacre of St. Bartholomew, in which uncounted thousands of Protestants died. The origins of this terrible event are uncertain, but they appear to rest in Catherine's resentment of a powerful Protestant noble, Gaspard de Coligny, who had a strong influence on her second son, Charles IX.

The Protestant nobility were gathered in Paris for the wedding of Margaret to Henry of Navarre, and here was a perfect opportunity to wipe out the Protestant leaders. Catherine seems to have induced her son to appoint a group of assassins to slay the Huguenot notables assembled for the wedding, sparing only Henry of Navarre and the Prince of Condé, another heir to the throne. Word of the plot spread among the populace, which was predominantly anti-Protestant. On the morning of August 24, St. Bartholomew's Day, when the bells in the church of St. Germain l'Auxerrois sounded, the Parisians rose in a fury and massacred Huguenots all over the city; before the day was over the Seine was running with the blood of thousands of dead. The slaughter of Paris set off a chain of other massacres all over France that went on until October. The Protestant party in France was not defeated; it was only roused to war.

A war of religion was in full sway in 1589, when the last of Catherine's sons died after an ineffectual reign. The Protestant Henry of Navarre was heir to the throne, but the French were not ready to accept him. They recognized the legitimacy of his claim, but they did not want a Huguenot. The Guise family, who headed the Catholic party, coveted the throne for themselves, and Henry of Navarre had to fight to secure it. He won it by valiant fighting and by renouncing his Protestantism. "Paris is worth a Mass," he is supposed to have said—a statement not so cynical as it has sometimes been portrayed, for Henry was mindful of his subjects' wishes and determined to give them national peace.

Having renounced Protestantism for himself, Henry brought the bloodshed over religion to an end in 1598 by the promulgation of the Edict of Nantes, which gave the Protestants legal recognition. It allowed them to hold secular offices, and it instituted special courts to see that they received justice. This was an edict promulgated not out of a conviction that men had the right to freedom of conscience, but because Henry had the vision to see that recognition was the only way to keep the peace. It arose out of the same principle that gave birth to the Peace of Augsburg in Germany: that the Church of Rome was no longer sovereign over all of Christendom. From now on secular statesmen rather than popes and prelates would define the values and order the direction of European society.

Everywhere in Europe the same movement was in process: in the Scandinavian countries, where the kings, like the German princes, used Lutheranism to consolidate their power; in Poland, where the Catholic faith became a nationalist bulwark against awakening Russia; in Hungary, where Calvinism and Catholicism joined to oppose Habsburg encroachment.

For the men who began the 16th Century in spiritual groping, the political result of the Reformation would probably have been appalling. The zeal of their cause had been put to a use they had not envisioned, and in the process had helped create hatreds and ambitions that were a far remove from the Christian virtues they had hoped to instill. In seeking to make men spiritual, Protestantism had succeeded in making them secular.

Even so, it had done much of what it had set out to do. In challenging and overcoming the rule of Rome, it had redistributed power in other hands—hands that were to become increasingly secular and increasingly middle class. Moreover, it had impelled the Church to re-examine itself. The Catholic Church was now to begin a reformation of its own.

A MONARCH ON THE MOVE, *Queen Elizabeth rides among her people in a fanciful open carriage, while an angelic herald proclaims her royal "fame."*

ELIZABETH'S ENGLAND

At a time when Europe was racked by religious struggles and rebellious discord, Queen Elizabeth successfully established a national Church and a secure monarchy in England. With political astuteness and womanly charm she managed to keep her subjects' attention directed toward her glittering court and the nation's prosperity rather than on their own bitter differences. To bolster England's security, the spinster Queen hinted at marriage to many of Europe's empire-hungry princes—but cleverly kept them all at arm's length. At the same time she built a navy that defeated Spain's feared Armada, giving England command of the seas. Elizabeth's court attracted a galaxy of brilliant commoners who, with equal talent, managed the government, laid claim to much of the New World and advanced the arts. Seen through the works of its contemporary artists, Elizabeth's colorful and growing England still stands as a "golden age."

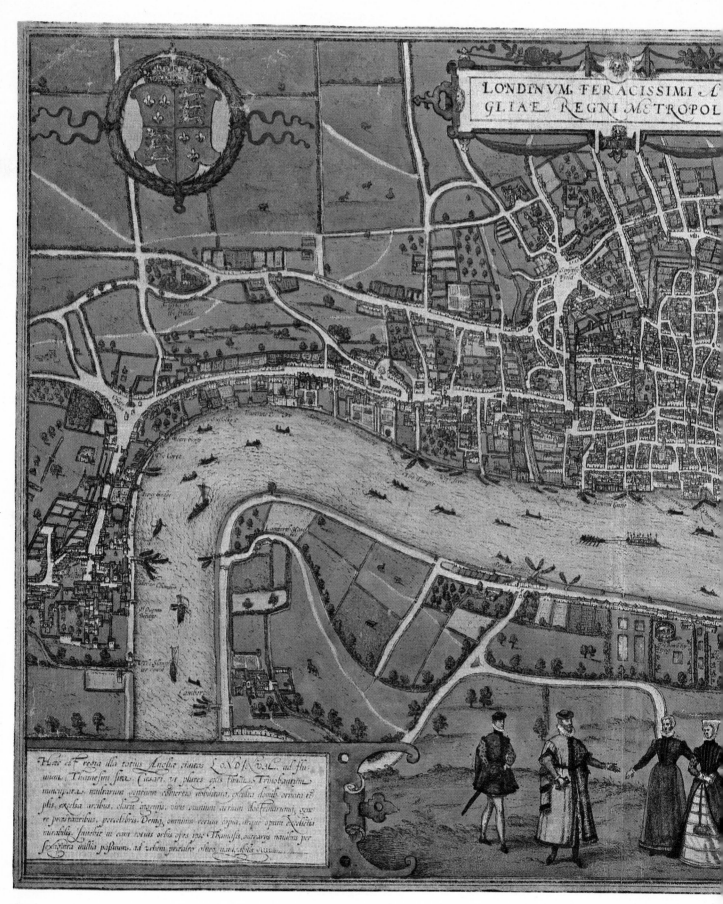

Elizabethan London: A City in Ferment

In Elizabeth's time few cities in the world rivaled London in size, influence or excitement. As this map executed in 1574 shows, the city was a maze of crooked streets and half-timbered houses, offset here and there with church spires, castles and the new mansions of the rich. Medieval walls curving back from the Tower of London along the Thames *(right)* defined the jurisdiction of the city proper, but its burgeoning population was rapidly spilling over into nearby farmland and confiscated monastic estates.

London drew people like a magnet: ambitious Englishmen from the countryside, Protestant refugees from the Continent, merchants seeking a commercial center free of European wars. In the course of Elizabeth's reign the population grew from 100,000 to nearly a quarter of a million. The result was such overcrowding that in 1598 one small-town visitor complained acidly of the city's "vast, unwieldy and disorderly Babel of buildings."

Amid all this growth and ferment, there flourished a new spirit of curiosity. Londoners who could read rummaged through the booksellers' stalls in St. Paul's churchyard to find passionate Italian sonnets, French novels, and tales of Raleigh's ill-fated Roanoke Colony. Thousands crossed the Thames every day to the Southwark theaters to see plays by Marlowe, Shakespeare and Jonson, or took boats upriver to Westminster's Star Chamber to witness political trials. Others crowded the Tower zoo to see four lions, a tiger and a porcupine; a camel was kept penned on London Bridge. In all, Elizabeth's city stood among the most cultured capitals of the world.

THE LORD MAYOR'S WIFE, *a commoner, walked through London with an almost queenly manner.*

A WEALTHY COUPLE *enjoys a promenade on horseba*

A WATER CARRIER *shoulders a barrel of fresh drinking water to dispense in the stre*

A SCHOLAR, *in cap and gown, favors an Elizabethan collar.*

A COUNTRY SQUIRE, *carrying a sack, rides his mule to town.*

GENTLEWOMAN *carries a feather fan, a popular part of the genteel wardrobe.*

ADIES OF THE COURT, *imitating the Queen, affected whisk collars and hooped skirts.*

A Society of Decorum and Ambition

Elizabeth presided over a social order which combined an older, feudal culture and a modern, middle-class world. Nearly everyone paid lip service to a rigid class system which set apart the nobles, gentry, yeomen and laborers. Laws prohibited a commoner from dressing up to pass as an aristocrat, and Shakespeare, himself a parvenu, predicted social catastrophe whenever "degree is shak'd."

Yet, despite the façade, Elizabethan society was remarkably fluid. Gentility no longer depended on inherited land and titles but was open to anyone who, a Privy Councillor observed, "can live idly and without manual labor, and will bear the port, charge, and countenance of a gentleman." More than ever before, self-made men dominated the London scene, as merchants, moneylenders and entrepreneurs climbed the ladder of success. Most got ahead by hard work and shrewd dealing: James Burbage, an itinerant actor, designed, financed and built London's first theater; Thomas Myddleton, a sugar dealer, made a fortune by investing in privateering expeditions against Spain. Some careers even had a fairy-tale touch: Edward Osborne, a poor lad apprenticed to a wealthy merchant, saved his patron's daughter from drowning in the Thames. Within a few years he had married her and, as London's Lord Mayor, was entertaining the Queen.

(Milites Provinciarum & Burgenses, (quos vocant) utrinq., qui Cameram Parlamenti inferiorem constituunt, Prolocutorem conducentes.

Prolocutor.

OPENING PARLIAMENT, _Elizabeth addresses her lords and bishops. In the foreground, members of the House of Commons look on from behind a railing._

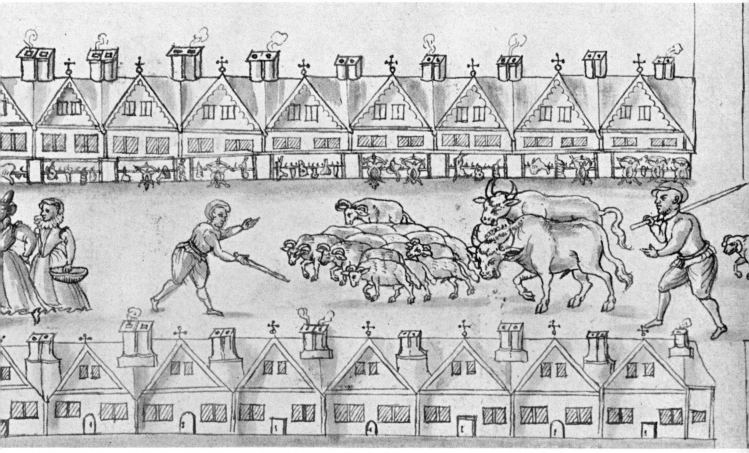

HERDING LIVESTOCK *into London's Eastcheap Street, lined with butcher shops, farmers bring their sheep and cattle to the city's main meat market.*

A Hub of Politics and Trade

All England seemed to find reasons to descend on Elizabeth's capital. The law courts, which opened only four times a year for three- to four-week terms, were swamped by throngs of attorneys and petitioners. When Parliament met *(far left)*, lords and gentry gathered from all over the realm to debate foreign policy, taxes and religion; many brought their wives, who spent lavish sums on the latest London styles, adding to an already prosperous commerce. Ships filled the city with exotic cargoes from European and Middle Eastern ports, while swarms of livestock in the markets provided tables with hearty local fare. London had become not only a prosperous city but an international marketplace.

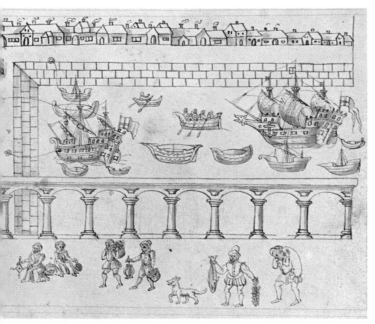

UNLOADING SHIPS *on the Thames, dockworkers carry fresh fish and sacks of goods from Billingsgate wharf. Many cargoes were sold directly on the dock.*

PALATIVM REGIVM IN ANGLI
Hoc est

Effigiauit Geovgius

Queenly "Progresses" through the Countryside

In most seasons, Elizabeth made London her home. But each summer she closed down her court and led the entire royal household on leisurely rambles, or "progresses," through the countryside as far as Derby, Dover and Bristol. During these sojourns of a month or two, she frequently made herself a guest on the great rural estates of her wealthier subjects, who

had to spend thousands of pounds entertaining her. At other times she stopped off to visit favorite country homes of her own. One of these was Nonsuch Palace *(above)*, near the forested deer chases of Surrey and Sussex. This regal estate was so named because, it was said, "there is nonsuch like it."

Whenever she traveled, Elizabeth rode on horseback or in an open carriage so she could be easily seen—and would extend a regal hand to all those crowding along the way. On these country excursions Elizabeth enjoyed a daily round of deer hunts, pageants, feasts and games. But she took even greater pleasure from mingling with farmers and country villagers, whose loyalty to the Crown became a priceless political asset.

Rough Entertainments
for a Royal Guest

Court life in London might be polished and decorous, but on her summer excursions Elizabeth preferred a less inhibited side of English life. Her presence invariably was the occasion for a round of country entertainments, including jousting, jugglers, tumblers, cockfights and animal acts. In her honor, villagers set up sporting events—which could be quite violent. One favorite game was a form of football which took a rugged toll among players. According to one contemporary account: "Sometimes their necks are broken, sometimes their backs . . . sometimes one part thrust out of joint. The best goeth not scot free but is sore wounded."

Nor, after the games, did the Queen's hosts spare the palates or paunches of the guests. At one feast the court was served 300 different dishes—and, so that "every man might feed on what he likes best," all of the main courses were set out at one time.

TILTING AT THE RING, *a resplendent country squire spurs his horse and tries to catch a dangling metal loop (left) with the point of his lance. The game developed from medieval jousting.*

COCKFIGHTING, *with roosters often fortified by brandy, was one of England's most popular betting sports. In this sketch by a Dutch artist, gentlemen crowd into a cockpit to watch a match.*

Het Haene gefecht Jn Engelandt,

5

THE "COUNTER REFORMATION"

As the tidal wave of Protestantism swept across 16th Century Europe, it seemed for a while that nothing would stop it from engulfing the whole continent. Northern Germany, Scandinavia and England, and parts of Poland, Hungary and Austria, were firmly Protestant. France was an uncertain bulwark, and even in Italy there were a few pangs of heretical doubt. But the Church of Rome was not standing idle in the face of the flood. Many dedicated Catholics submitted their Church to rigorous examination and campaigned diligently for improvement. Their labor produced a massive reform that revitalized the Church. By mid-century, Rome had not only stemmed the Protestant tide but had re-established itself as a dynamic force in European affairs.

This remarkable recovery is often called by historians the Counter Reformation, but the name means more than it says. What happened to the Church at this time was, assuredly, in part a reaction against the onslaught of Protestantism. But actually the Church's reform began at the end of the 15th Century, long before Luther published his 95 Theses, and its progress over the next 80 years was spurred as much by internal pressure as by the threat from without. It was initiated by Churchmen who were as concerned about the failures of the Renaissance Church as Luther was to become. It took shape as a grassroots reform movement, spearheaded by zealous new monastic groups; it was given direction by a renovated papacy that belatedly faced up to its responsibilities. Finally, at mid-century, the reform was articulated and cemented by one of the most important events in the history of the Church, the Council of Trent.

The seedbed for this Catholic reformation was Spain, whose peculiar social and political heritage fitted it for a special role. First, of course, the Pyrenees made an effective natural barrier to any infectious ideas that might come down from Europe. But more important, Spain was the one country in western Europe that contained a sizable non-Christian population. There had been Jews and Moors living in Spain for centuries, making significant commercial and cultural contributions to the country. Over the years many of them had already been Christianized, often under duress, but fear and

JESUITS IN FULL PANOPLY, *attended by cardinals and Pope Urban VIII, celebrate their Society's 1639 centennial amid the baroque splendors of Rome's Il Gesù church (seen in a cutaway view from the carriage-thronged street).*

jealousy of the Marranos and Moriscos, as converted Jews and Moors were called, kept animosity alive.

In 1480 Ferdinand and Isabella, struggling for national and religious unity and sparked by their ambition for an absolute monarchy, established the Inquisition, a powerful tribunal charged with suppressing heresy and unorthodoxy. It acted in the name of the Church, but it also functioned as an arm of the state, an instrument to continue in up-to-date fashion the age-old holy war against the infidel. (Not for another 40 years would Protestant heretics come under its cold scrutiny.)

Inquisitional fervor, which inevitably led to religious intolerance and cruel repression, also led to religious reform. Vigorous Church leaders finally became alarmed by the depth of the ignorance of some priests who did not understand the Latin of the Mass, and by the moral laxity that permitted monks to keep concubines and clerics to operate outside businesses such as taverns and even brothels. The Churchmen realized that to succeed in the war on heresy they would have to start by cleaning out their own house.

The first to take significant action was Francisco Jiménez de Cisneros, the son of a noble family, who studied law and theology and went to Rome to serve in the papal court. After a routine career as an ecclesiastical administrator he suddenly decided at the age of 48 to join the Franciscan Order and assume an ascetic existence of sanctity and self-denial. His fervent spiritualism came to the notice of Queen Isabella, who was herself ardently religious, and she made him her confessor. By 1495 he had become the Archbishop of Toledo and, next to the monarchs, the most powerful man in Spain.

As Archbishop, and later as a Cardinal, Jiménez devoted his last 20 years to reform and education of the clergy. He cleansed the monasteries of corruption, pursued recalcitrant monks with all the force of the law and—as a last resort—banished incorrigi-

A POLYGLOT BIBLE, *published in 1522 by Spain's Alcalá University, reflects Catho* *scholars' broadening interest in ancient languages. On the page shown above is* *passage from Genesis in four versions (left to right): Greek, with an interline* *Latin translation; the official Latin Vulgate text; the Hebrew original; and (acro* *the bottom) an Aramaic paraphrase of the Hebrew, with its own Latin translatio*

bles to lonely service among the infidels in Morocco. He even imprisoned members of the higher clergy who resisted him.

Through all his years of power Jiménez shaped his own life with the austerity and strict morality of his days as a monk. It is said that when Pope Alexander VI enjoined Jiménez to wear the luxurious robes that befitted a prelate of his station, Jiménez reluctantly complied, but underneath the finery he wore his Franciscan habit and under that a hair shirt.

For all his asceticism, Jiménez was touched by the humanism of the times and appreciated the importance of education. In 1500 he established the University of Alcalá, which soon attained such eminence that Spaniards proudly called it the eighth wonder of the world. The reforms achieved by Jiménez were so effective that when he died in 1517 the Spanish Church rested on a moral foundation of iron, and Luther was yet to fire his opening shot. Had Jiménez done his work in Germany instead of Spain, Luther might never have been heard from.

The other stronghold of Catholicism was, of course, Italy. Here, as in Spain, there were strong social and political reasons why Lutheranism and Calvinism failed to gain the firm foothold they had so quickly attained in the north. Most prosperous Italians were secularly and humanistically inclined and found little in the dour doctrines of the north to inspire a transfer of allegiance; they also saw in Catholicism a buttress of social order. The peasantry, for its part, remained solidly attached to the old faith and its traditions. And it must be remembered that the papacy, while often derided by Italians, was a cherished national institution—and the source of great wealth which few cared to see destroyed. All these factors militated against the overthrow of the Church and in favor of reform from within.

In Italy reform came later than in Spain, and from a different direction. The impetus came not from the top, but largely from new monastic groups motivated by a compulsion to spread their religion and good works among the people. First among these was the Oratory of Divine Love, founded in Rome in 1517 as a pious brotherhood dedicated to prayer, self-reform and service to the poor. From the start this group gave inspiration and example to other orders.

The most vigorous of these was the Order of the Capuchins, an offshoot of the Franciscans determined to restore the strict monastic rule which had been laid down by St. Francis and since forgotten. Organized in 1528, the Capuchins—so named because they adopted *capucini*, or hoods, such as that worn by St. Francis—devoted themselves to teaching and preaching among the poor, to tending the sick, and to setting an example of piety, austerity and unworldliness for the faithful to follow.

Other orders initiated in this time of renewed fervor were the Theatines, dedicated to service among the poor, and from whose ranks were to come more than 200 bishops; the Ursulines, an order of women founded in 1535 and dedicated to the teaching of girls and the care of the sick and the poor; and the Fathers of the Oratory, an association of priests founded in Rome around 1540, who preached and sang religious music at various churches and country greens.

In Spain the spirit of reform that had inspired Jiménez was also reaching down to the people. The most luminous figure in this movement of popular piety was Teresa of Avila, later to become a patron saint of Spain. A nobleman's daughter who became a sister in the Carmelite Order, Teresa was for years troubled by convulsive seizures. After one long sickness during which she was partially paralyzed, she suddenly and inexplicably recovered, and afterward experienced mystical trances and ecstatic visions. She interpreted these as a manifestation of divine will and dedicated herself to restoring the vigor of monastic life.

Finding the comfortable existence of the Carmelites too lax and self-indulgent, she broke away from the order in 1562 and established a convent of her own. Here she gathered a small band of nuns who shared her spiritual zeal; they wore simple robes and rope sandals, and led lives of unadorned piety. This group, which became a new order called the Discalced (shoeless) Carmelites, aroused the resentment of less austere monks and nuns, but Teresa persevered in her campaign to revive the religious spirit. With serene determination she eventually founded 30 convents in her order.

A Spaniard of a more practical, hardheaded temper forged an even more decisive weapon in the campaign of Catholic renewal. He was Ignatius of Loyola, who in 1540 founded the Society of Jesus, a group of priests later to be called the Jesuits, who spearheaded the Church's reform movement and stamped it with their character.

In his early career there was little to suggest the singular role that Ignatius would be called on to play. As a young Basque nobleman with red hair and lively eyes, Ignatius had been rowdy and lusty, much given to dueling and carousing. His imagination had fed upon the courtly romances of valorous knights and beautiful ladies that formed the popular reading fare of the day. Dreaming of grandeur and conquests of his own, he embarked on the life of a soldier in Spanish Navarre in 1517. Four years later, in a battle at Pamplona, his dreams collapsed when a cannon blast shattered one leg, leaving him crippled for life.

While convalescing he asked for books, but the only two he could find were one describing the lives of the saints and another recounting the life of Christ. These stirred his imagination with possibilities for another kind of fame and glory. In true chivalric fashion he determined to emulate the saints in service to the Virgin by becoming a soldier of Christ.

Then followed an anxious year of prayer, penance and prolonged meditation, during which Ignatius experienced a series of mystical visions. From this intense soul-searching he emerged with a deep sense of a mission in life and an unshakable conviction that God would lead him. This religious experience ultimately found expression in the *Spiritual Exercises*, a manual of self-discipline designed to guide the individual toward the control of his will and emotions and the subordination of his bodily desires to the needs of the spirit. Though the work is neither stylistically eloquent nor theologically profound, its explicit directions and psychological soundness have provided spiritual inspiration for Catholics for four centuries.

After a pilgrimage to Jerusalem, Ignatius decided in 1524 that he needed greater learning. Though he was in his thirties, he enrolled in school in Barcelona, where he sat on rude benches with schoolboys, hunched over grammar books, learning Latin. After this he studied for 10 years in various universities in Spain and Paris.

Everywhere he went, his intense convictions and enthusiasm for converting souls made him enemies; altogether he was charged with heresy and acquitted 10 times by an Inquisition made nervous by Lutheranism and suspicious of anyone whose behavior was out of the ordinary. But everywhere his passionate devotion and good works also drew men to him.

In Paris Ignatius gathered his first permanent disciples. Here, in August of 1534, he and six friends met in the tiny chapel of St. Denis on the slopes of Montmartre and vowed to pursue a life of poverty and celibacy. They also pledged to go to Rome and submit themselves to the Pope for whatever task he might command. In this way was born what Ignatius called the "Company of Jesus."

In Rome the little band of priests faced powerful opposition and the same kind of suspicion that had dogged Ignatius before. But in September 1540, Pope Paul III, persuaded that Ignatius was trustworthy, gave him and his followers official sanction, ratifying their aims in the bull *Regimini militantis ecclesiae* ("For the Rule of the Church Militant"). Thus the Society of Jesus was formed and Ignatius was elected its head, or General.

For 15 years, until his death, he led the Jesuits in a spectacular crusade to defend and propagate the faith throughout the world. More than any other group they symbolized a new attitude that was to pervade the Church, one of militant reform. With disciplined fervor they undertook a wide variety of endeavors that ranged from public preaching and works of charity to the education of the young, the conversion of heathens, and the combating of heresy.

To accomplish these tasks the Jesuits developed a uniquely efficient organization, in which all other considerations—including the ascetic and otherworldly—were subordinated to the overriding need to get things done. Instituted along the military lines Ignatius had learned as a young man, the Society imposed a rigid discipline on all its members, who were for all practical purposes under the absolute domination of the General.

Obedience, in fact, was the great watchword of Ignatius. For the medieval monk obedience had meant withdrawal from the world into a cloistered asceticism; for Ignatius it meant service through an active life in the world. And in his campaign he did not want to be distracted by abstract theological questions. "To arrive at the truth in all things," he wrote in the *Spiritual Exercises*, "we ought always to be ready to believe that what seems to us white is black, if the hierarchical Church so defines it." In other words, the good Christian was to accept unquestioningly whatever God demanded, as interpreted by the Church.

In this spirit of obedience, the Jesuits undertook one of their most fruitful activities, one admirably suited to the tremendous expansion of the earth's frontiers in the 16th Century. This was the missionary enterprise they launched throughout the world—in Africa, India, the Far East and in the newly discovered Americas.

They recruited hundreds of missionaries, but undoubtedly the best known is St. Francis Xavier, a Spaniard who, like Ignatius, had given up a gay life of aristocratic indulgence and who had been one of the original Company of Jesus. In 1540, when King John III of Portugal asked for missionaries to convert the heathen peoples the Portuguese had discovered in India, Ignatius chose Xavier.

Through the next 11 years Xavier carried the message of the Church beyond India to Ceylon, Malaya, the East Indies and Japan. Everywhere he went he converted the multitudes by means of simple sermons preached in the native tongue, and he baptized children and adults by the tens of thousands. When Xavier died in 1552 on an island in the South China Sea, other Jesuit missionaries were already carrying the faith to the heathen not only in Asia but in Brazil, Ethiopia, the Congo and Morocco.

The Jesuits played their greatest role in the realm of education. Ignatius understood that if the members of his order were to lead the forces of Catholicism in the struggle for men's minds, they must be well trained not only as clerics but as scholars. Finding the existing colleges insufficient for his needs, he established dozens of schools for Jesuit seminarians. Gradually the fame of the Jesuits as teachers spread, and they were asked to take over the direction of existing universities. By 1600 four fifths of the Jesuits were teachers, and they controlled hundreds of schools and colleges. By the middle of the 17th Century the Jesuits were educating virtually all of Catholic Europe. Through this activity they assured the recovery and expan-

ROMA.

sion of the Catholic religion in formerly doubtful territory.

The key to this success was, as in all Jesuit enterprises, discipline and thoroughness. Before a Jesuit walked into a classroom to teach he had had almost 10 years of concentrated instruction from other Jesuits in philosophy, theology, mathematics, Latin, Greek, Hebrew, rhetoric and the classics. The regimen by which he taught others called for frequent examinations, rigid discipline and continuous supervision, but it also adapted the methods of humanism. It reversed time-honored tradition by prohibiting any Jesuit from administering physical punishment to his students. Understanding the importance of motivation, Jesuit teachers enlivened the curriculum with competitions and prizes, and

they encouraged friendly rivalry among students.

Many of the Jesuits' techniques were borrowed from existing practice. What they brought to education was organization combined with the zeal of men serving a cause. Pervading all their teaching was an unwavering emphasis on moral discipline and religious instruction. All students had to attend Mass every day; once a week they heard a sermon and an uplifting lecture in Latin. By the time a Jesuit-taught scholar went out into the world he was not only thoroughly educated, but thoroughly indoctrinated in the glory of the Church of Rome.

The Pope who commissioned Ignatius Loyola in his crusade was Paul III, and his pontificate, beginning in 1534, marked a turning point in the history of the Church; for the first time the long-building movement of reform found effective leadership in the Vatican.

Paul III was a transition figure whose roots were in the Renaissance but whose spirit was sympathetic to the need for reform. Born Alexander Farnese in 1468, he had been educated at the court of Lorenzo the Magnificent in Florence and he well represented in his tastes, habits and ambitions all the virtues and vices of his Renaissance predecessors. At 25 he had been raised to the cardinalate even before becoming a priest, and before his election to the papacy he had produced four bastard children whose political careers and preferments were a continuous embarrassment to his pontificate. Yet if he was not free from nepotism, Paul was nonetheless a man of ability and of great culture (it was he who commissioned Michelangelo to paint the *Last Judgment* in the Sistine Chapel). He recognized in the instability of the European scene the grave threat posed both to the papacy and to the unity of the Church, and with it the pressing need for action to infuse new vigor into the Church. Paul III was also stubborn and bad tempered enough to get his way.

He started his campaign for reform with the Curia, whose conservative character he gradually changed by promoting to the cardinalate reform-minded men of integrity. He next appointed a commission of nine cardinals to investigate the condition of the Church. Their report, which Paul called the *aureum consilium,* or "golden counsel," was submitted in 1537 and constituted a comprehensive catalogue of all the abuses of the Church. It criticized the appointment of unworthy men to ecclesiastical office; the unsavory traffic in benefices, indulgences and dispensations; and the Curia's failure to discharge its duties. Finally, the committee denounced the "reckless exaggeration of the papal authority" as a source of these evil practices

and as a prime cause of the Lutheran defections.

Paul made a start in effecting the drastic reforms the report proposed. Though he met strong opposition, he tried to put an end to episcopal absenteeism by demanding that bishops reside in their dioceses. He chartered the Jesuit Order in 1540 and in 1542 he established the Roman Inquisition to stamp out heresy. But the real significance of his pontificate lies in the convening of the Council of Trent, which finally put an official seal on the Church's reform movement. Because of various interruptions, it would be another 20 years before this enterprise could accomplish its goal, but in the meantime the transformation of the papacy from a circus to a seat of morality was completed. Chiefly responsible was Paul IV, who had been Gian Pietro Caraffa, a founder of the Theatines and one of Paul III's ablest cardinals.

Paul IV had a passion for reform that shook the Church to its roots. An acquaintance wrote, "The Pope is a man of iron, and the very stones over which he walks emit sparks." With stern purpose and unrelenting energy, he completed the renovation of the Curia. He worked zealously to improve clerical morals, and he brought to an end the practice of nepotism by unhesitatingly firing from the cardinalate two of his own relatives who were accused of corrupt behavior.

Paul IV also applied his zeal to stamping out heresy, but here his fervor carried him to extremes that troubled his pontificate and sullied his reputation. As a Cardinal he had led the Inquisition under Paul III; now he decreed that it "was in no case to employ gentleness," and soon the Inquisition became the terror of Rome. Pitilessly it pursued everyone suspected of unorthodox behavior, and Paul IV unfailingly attended the weekly Thursday meetings of the Inquisition tribunal to see that there was no leniency. When he died in 1559, the rabble of Rome reacted to the end of his oppressive reign by rioting happily in the streets, destroying the headquarters of the Inquisition and throwing the Pope's statue into the Tiber.

A gentler man, Pius IV, succeeded Paul IV, and under him the Council of Trent finally completed the great work of reform from within. The Council had had its troubles from the beginning. Paul III had determined to call it in 1537, but he and Emperor Charles V argued for years over its location, and finally compromised on Trent as a town that was technically in the Empire but virtually part of Italy. Political turbulence in Europe, further quarrels between Charles and Paul III, a threat of plague, and Paul IV's involvement in his personal reform campaign caused repeated delays and adjournments. When the Council finally adjourned for the last time in 1563, it had been in being for 18 years, but had actually been in working session only four and a half years.

Attending the Council's sessions were Churchmen of high rank, mostly from Italy, Spain, France and Germany, who sometimes numbered as few as 60, sometimes more than 250. Though the prelates varied widely in opinion and purpose—the records tell of more than one heated, beard-pulling squabble between bishops—they were all Catholics, except for a few Protestants who appeared at some early sessions. There was some optimism, at first, that the Council might reunite the Church, but the hope was vain; by the time of Trent the Protestant revolution had gone too far for conciliation. What the Council of Trent did do was subject all Catholic dogma and practice to the most searching scrutiny in the history of the Church. The result of this examination was an unambiguous reaffirmation of almost every doctrine challenged by the Protestants.

Whereas Luther said that Scripture is the only true authority for doctrine, Trent decreed Church tradition to be equally authoritative and reasserted for the Church the exclusive right to interpret the Scriptures. On the matter of justification by faith, the Council agreed that faith is necessary for salvation, but refuted Luther by insisting that man can also help earn his own way with good works and participation in the sacraments. It also confirmed the efficacy of indulgences granted by the Church to remit the penance required for sins.

The Churchmen at Trent applied themselves to practical matters of reform as well as to doctrine. They forbade the clergy to receive money for personal gain in return for granting indulgences, and warned against superstition in the veneration of saints and relics. They provided for an Index of books forbidden to Catholics. Even today Catholic authors writing on matters of doctrine submit their works to ecclesiastical review for the *nihil obstat* ("nothing conflicts") and *imprimatur* ("it may be printed") that certify their orthodoxy—a legacy from Trent.

The most far-reaching action taken by the Council was to define the authority and responsibilities of the bishops. No longer could absentee bishops collect the incomes from their benefices while enjoying the good life in Rome. The burden of parochial reform was placed on their shoulders, thus assuring that reform would reach down to the lowest level. Furthermore the Council reflected the day's concern with education by requiring that every bishop establish in his diocese a theological seminary for the training of priests, so that the much-criticized ignorance of Churchmen should be exorcised. In this foresighted action the Council ensured that the reforms so laboriously won over the previous half-century would be perpetuated by a disciplined and enlightened clergy.

Thus the Church of Rome survived the Reformation. Its domain was now limited and the division of Christendom remained unhealed, but as a result of its ordeal, Catholicism was stronger than ever before.

THE COUNCIL OF TRENT, *a group of bishops which met from 1545 to 1563, sought to define Church dogma.*

THE CHURCH FIGHTS BACK

As Protestantism swept triumphantly over almost all of northern and central Europe (even in Italy, whole towns threatened to defect), the Catholic Church took decisive steps to combat its enemies and to reform itself. During the Counter Reformation leading theologians met in neutral territory just north of Italy at the Council of Trent *(above)* to hammer out clear statements of orthodox belief. Missionaries swept through Asia, Africa and the Americas and won hordes of converts. A strict new order of priests, the Jesuits, preached and taught in their own colleges with such fervor that soon they won back to Catholicism most of the people of Poland and many of those who had left the Church in Germany, Hungary and Bohemia. Gone were the days of cynical, pleasure-loving Renaissance popes; now the Church was ruled by stern men like Paul IV, who said, "Even if my own father were a heretic, I would gather wood to burn him."

THE VIRGIN TRIUMPHANT *kneels between Christ and a banner extolling her virtues, in a fresco by Il Domenichino. Below her a girl symbolizing Prayer hol...*

SEMPER VIRGO DEI GENITRIX IMMACVLATA

rosary, and a Catholic hero treads a defeated Luther and Calvin underfoot.

CHRIST CRUCIFIED *is borne to heaven by God in a work by El Greco.*

The Testimony of Art

In its struggles against heresy, Catholicism called upon its artists. When Protestants attacked the veneration of Mary as idolatry, Catholic painters responded with paintings honoring her. When some radical thinkers rejected the doctrine of the Trinity, artists such as El Greco produced magnificent works depicting the Father, the Son and, in the form of a dove, the Holy Ghost *(above)*. Pagan deities were excluded from Church art, and in a new wave of Church-inspired modesty, even some of Michelangelo's nude figures in the Sistine Chapel frescoes were painted over with clothes.

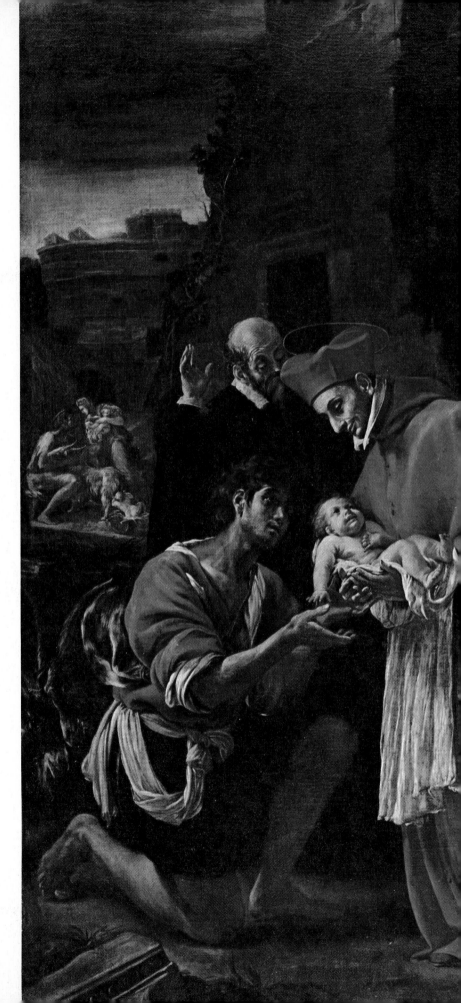

A Call to Sanctity and Service

Catholic reform leaders passionately embraced an ideal of the humble, pious life. Before the Counter Reformation Pope Leo X was said to have remarked cynically, "All the world knows how profitable this fable of Christ has been to us and ours." Now Churchmen sought to prove their sincerity. St. Charles Borromeo *(right)* and Gian Pietro Caraffa (later Pope Paul IV) gave all their wealth to the poor. Such aristocrats as St. Ignatius and St. Teresa of Avila begged for food while tending the needs of others. New orders—the Capuchin monks, the Theatines, Barnabites and Jesuits—took vows of poverty and chastity and poured their energies into creating hospitals and schools.

Church officials ordered monks to give up their concubines and bishops to keep frugal tables. In 1547 the dark confessional box was introduced, so priests might no longer be tempted by beautiful penitents. In Spain this religious zeal went to such lengths that soon nearly one quarter of the population was enrolled in monasteries.

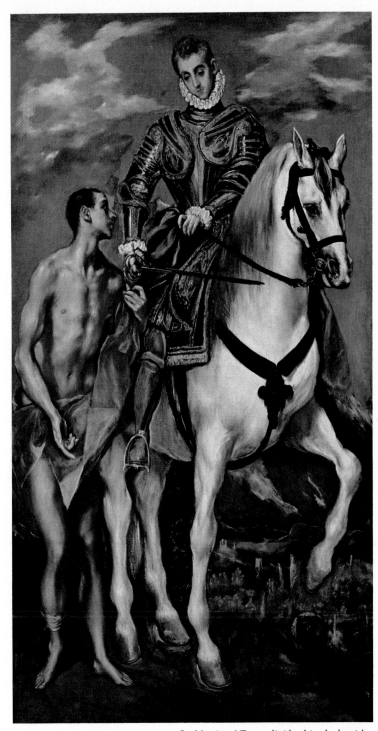

A MODEL OF CHARITY, *St. Martin of Tours divides his cloak with a beggar in a 16th Century canvas by El Greco. The word "chapel" derives from the Italian word for St. Martin's cloak, "cappella."*

TENDING THE SICK, *St. Charles Borromeo comforts a child struck by the plague of 1576. While others fled Milan, the city's archbishop stayed bravely behind—and lived for eight more years.*

Propagating the Faith among the Heathen

The Jesuits were the most successful Catholic missionaries, frequently because of an ability to adapt Christianity to local customs. In India, Robert de Nobili became a vegetarian and proclaimed Christianity as a Veda, or Hindu scripture. In China, Matteo Ricci wore mandarin robes and permitted converts to continue ancestor worship.

In Japan, Jesuits stressed Christian rituals that paralleled local ceremonies for the dead; thousands of converts were made. But in 1596 a Spanish captain insulted the Japanese emperor. The enraged sovereign arrested the missionaries—and, drawing a leaf from their Bible, had them crucified.

A PORTUGUESE JESUIT, *painted by a Japanese artist, stands beside two Japanese Christian children.*

PROPOSING A TEST, *two Jesuits (left), at the court of a Mohammedan prince in India, offer to enter the fire with the Bible in hand if the Mohammedans will do the same while clasping the Koran.*

A MINGLING OF CULTURES *occurs as Jesuits, Franciscans and a Japanese delegation (right) meet a group of European merchants. In the distance a priest and a convert worship at a Christian altar.*

115

A Sudden Outburst of Violence

During the first half of the 16th Century, most of the conflicts between Catholics and Protestants were purely verbal. But after 1550, blood was shed in religious battles all over Europe. In France the tensions that had been developing between Catholics and Calvinists (called Huguenots) were trig-

gered by a political power play and culminated in 1572 in the gory Massacre of St. Bartholomew. This slaughter of Protestants by Catholics began in Paris on August 24, the feast day of St. Bartholomew; a Huguenot artist, François Dubois, lived to execute this painting of the event. The strife spread to the provinces, and in six weeks more than 10,000 Huguenots were killed. The Protestant leader, Admiral Coligny, was decapitated (right center), and his head was sent to Rome. There Pope Gregory XIII received it joyfully, and struck a commemorative medal celebrating this latest Catholic triumph.

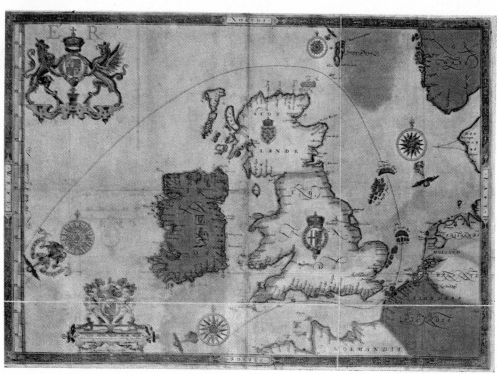

THE ARMADA'S ROUTE, *traced in a contemporary engraving, shows the course the Spanish fleet followed into the English Channel. After four major encounters, the defeated Armada went home by way of Ireland.*

THE VICTORIOUS MONARCH *Elizabeth I rides a white charger while the Spanish Armada, surrounded by the English fleet, burns in the distance. This symbolic scene was painted on wood—believed to be from an Armada vessel demolished on the coast of Scotland.*

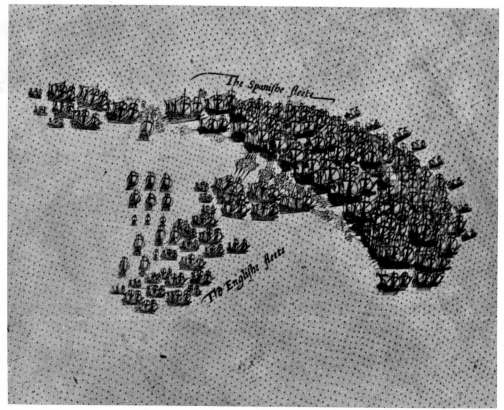

IN THE FIRST ENGAGEMENT, *Spanish and English ships clash near Plymouth. The Armada sought to envelop the English in its crescent formation, but English ships were too nimble to be caught in the trap.*

An Encounter between Two True Faiths

When Philip II sent the Spanish Armada in 1588 to assist in an attempted invasion of England, he saw the invasion as a holy crusade to force Protestant England to return to the Catholic Church. Astrologers had long predicted that the year would hold ominous events; one of the Armada's top officers, when asked how the Spanish hoped to defeat the superior English fleet, replied, "we are sailing against England in the confident hope of a miracle."

The English also believed that God was on their side. During the final decisive clash between the two fleets a sudden squall scattered the attacking fleet. The Armada limped home and England proclaimed, "God breathed and they were scattered."

The Religious War That Exhausted Europe

From 1618 to 1648 the Protestant princes of Germany, supported by Denmark and Sweden, fought against the Catholic Habsburgs and their allies for the survival of Protestantism in the Empire. The Habsburgs, who ruled Spain, Austria, the Spanish Netherlands and most of Germany and Italy, were the stanchest defenders of the papacy. France, though Catholic, fought the Habsburgs, and one of the most decisive battles was a French victory at Rocroi *(right)*. There the French commander, the Duc d'Enghien (shown on the white horse at center), smashed the "invincible" Spanish infantry.

When the Thirty Years' War ended, politics was at last disentangled from religion. In Germany the major denominations now lived in relative peace. The truce also ended the Pope's political power. Sensing this defeat, Pope Innocent X declared the treaty "null, void, invalid, iniquitous, unjust, damnable, reprobate, inane, empty of meaning and effect for all times." He was met with polite silence.

6

A REVOLUTION IN LETTERS

Never before the 16th Century had men been so intoxicated with the power of the written word; never before had the written word reached so many men. Printing made it possible; Reformation furor and Renaissance élan combined to accelerate it.

By a curious paradox, Germany led all Europe in printing but lagged in writing. Most German thinkers of the century spent their energies on the religious quarrel, and their ideas found expression in tracts and pamphlets. But the major contributions to 16th Century letters were made by France, Spain and England—and although all these countries had printers, the German cities of Strasbourg, Augsburg, Nuremberg, Wittenberg, Cologne, Leipzig, Frankfort and Magdeburg provided much of the printing for the rest of Europe.

In some measure the Reformation was a reaction against the Renaissance; yet the reformers were themselves indebted to the revival they spurned. For it was the Renaissance acquaintance with Greek that led to the re-examination of the early versions of the Scriptures, which in turn enabled the reformers to examine religious beliefs. And in the end Renaissance humanism reasserted itself— not in Germany, but in France and England. The result was a revolution in the literature of Europe. Preoccupation with the Greek and Latin classics gave way to writings in the vernacular; religious fervor was superseded by secularism; and literacy, once the monopoly of the scholarly elite, spread to the people.

The author who most vividly reflected this intellectual ferment at its outset was Erasmus—witty, urbane and scholarly, called by a friend the "glory of our age." More than any other man in the early 16th Century, Erasmus articulated the failings of the Church and society, and he did much to generate the movement that the reformers carried out.

Erasmus put his own hand to nearly every subject and to several of the genres that marked 16th Century literature—theology and social criticism, translation, poetry and satire. His greatest original work was the *Encomium moriae*, translated as *The Praise of Folly*, but in Erasmus' Latin a *double-entendre* that also gave praise to his friend Sir Thomas More.

The Praise of Folly is an artful vision of the ab-

THE CREATION OF THE WORLD, *by an anonymous artist—one of 124 woodcuts in Luther's 1534 Bible—depicts an elaborately vested God presiding over the new earth. Luther's translation not only gave people an understandable version of the Scriptures, but helped establish modern vernacular German.*

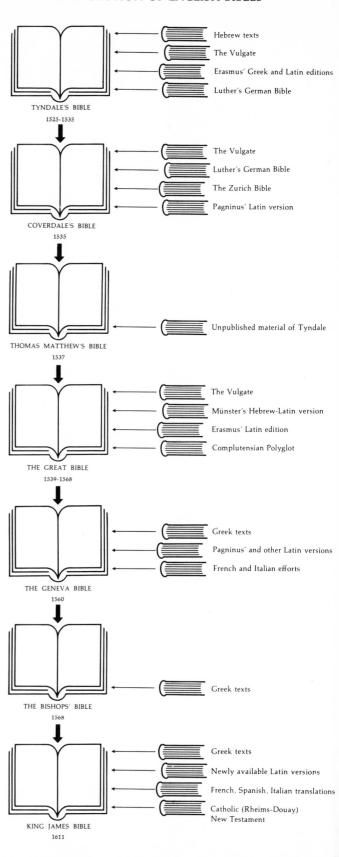

THE EVOLUTION OF ENGLISH BIBLES

TYNDALE'S BIBLE
1525-1535

Hebrew texts
The Vulgate
Erasmus' Greek and Latin editions
Luther's German Bible

COVERDALE'S BIBLE
1535

The Vulgate
Luther's German Bible
The Zurich Bible
Pagninus' Latin version

THOMAS MATTHEW'S BIBLE
1537

Unpublished material of Tyndale

THE GREAT BIBLE
1539-1568

The Vulgate
Münster's Hebrew-Latin version
Erasmus' Latin edition
Complutensian Polyglot

THE GENEVA BIBLE
1560

Greek texts
Pagninus' and other Latin versions
French and Italian efforts

THE BISHOPS' BIBLE
1568

Greek texts

KING JAMES BIBLE
1611

Greek texts
Newly available Latin versions
French, Spanish, Italian translations
Catholic (Rheims-Douay) New Testament

surdity of human behavior, a brilliant jest combining fancy and soberness, in which Folly, addressing mankind, asserts that she is useful—indeed, essential—to life. "Without me," she says, "the world cannot exist for a moment. For is not all that is done . . . among mortals full of folly; is it not performed by fools and for fools?"

Folly, says Erasmus, is the antithesis of reason; it is evil delusion, responsible for war and worldliness, for all the ills of life. Yet folly makes life sufferable. "No society, no cohabitation can be pleasant or lasting without folly; so much so that a people could not stand its prince, nor the master his man, nor the maid her mistress, nor the tutor his pupil, nor the friend his friend, nor the wife her husband for a moment longer if they did not now and then err together, now flatter each other; now sensibly conniving at things, now smearing themselves with some honey of folly."

Folly surveys the whole range of human behavior: love and sacrifice, courage and cowardice, reason and madness, statesmanship and scholarship. She deals sharply with all phases of society, but she is particularly hard on the Church. She pokes fun at theologians, who "will tell you to a tittle all the successive proceedings of Omnipotence in the creation of the universe"; at miracles, shrines, indulgences, monks and cardinals; at popes, who in the "riches, honors, jurisdictions, offices" they covet and the "ceremonies . . . excommunications and interdicts" they indulge in, have lost all resemblance to the Apostles they are supposed to represent.

Perhaps Erasmus' greatest accomplishment—and certainly the one that had the broadest ramifications—was his compilation of the early Greek Gospels and Epistles of the New Testament, which he published in 1516 together with a new Latin translation of his own.

For its challenge to orthodoxy, the work electrified the theological world as soon as it appeared, drawing praise from the humanists and latent reformers, and merciless attack from others. Luther used Erasmus' text when he lectured to his students at Wittenberg, and when he translated the Bible into German, it was from Erasmus' Bible that he worked. In England William Tyndale, an English admirer of Erasmus, used the same version when he translated the Bible into English—and Tyndale's version was, in turn, the cornerstone of the King James Version. Whether they used Erasmus' Bible or not, men all over Europe carried Erasmus' idea a step further, and before the century was over they had translated the Bible into almost every language of Europe.

Indeed, a veritable fever for translation overtook Europe in the 16th Century. It was not confined to the Bible, but extended as well to philosophical treatises, poetry, histories and plays.

John Calvin was the first to write a scholarly treatise in a modern language. He originally wrote his *Institutes of the Christian Religion* in Latin—in order, he said, that it might reach the learned of all lands. Five years later, wishing to reach the faithful among his countrymen, he translated it into French. Calling on his training in logic and law, he wrote in a style that was simple and direct, and he initiated the lucidity that to this day characterizes the French language.

The next step was to write in French to begin with. This practice was not actually a product of the 16th Century; the French had been writing poetry, romances and comic tales in their own language since medieval times. But with the influx of Renaissance ideals from Italy, the French began to graft classic rhetoric and vocabulary onto their own language, and to use French, thus fortified, for serious subjects. Once this began to happen, France witnessed an upwelling of literary activity, combining both medieval and Renaissance elements. The movement culminated in the lusty works of one of the great figures in French literature, François Rabelais.

Rabelais was born about 1494, in Touraine, the son of a well-to-do lawyer who placed François in a Franciscan monastery when he was about 17. Even as an adolescent he exhibited a voracious curiosity and a boisterous spirit that the monastery could not contain. He detested the ignorance and simplicity of the monks who were his companions, and he studied the classics with such fervor that he was urged by his superiors to desist; when he did not, he was confined to his cell and deprived of his books. He subsequently left monastic life and roved through France and Italy, dabbling in this and that; by the time he reached his middle years he had done turns as a monk, a secular priest, a physician and an editor, and had acquired a vast store of knowledge that ranged over law, theology, history, botany, anatomy, astronomy, mythology and cuisine.

In the 1530s an anonymous author committed to print the tales of a legendary folk hero common to many areas of France, a benevolent giant named Gargantua, who had an appetite for food, women and derring-do commensurate with his oversized body. Rabelais may have been the author of this work; whether he was or not, the thought struck him that of this little volume "more copies would be sold in two months than people would buy Bibles in nine years," and so he turned to composing a fanciful tale about the giant's son, Pantagruel. He later went back to pick up Gargantua and even his ancestors, and the work was eventually expanded to five volumes.

In Rabelais' version Gargantua is a philosopher-king who reigns over a state for which Rabelais took his inspiration from Plato's *Republic*. The son, Pantagruel, reflecting the growth of learning and contemporary reverence for it, outdoes his father in erudition and ability.

One of the book's major characters is a jolly monk, Friar John, through whom Rabelais satirizes all the charges that the reformers leveled against the monks—their indolence, greed, lust and lack of attention to prayer. "I never sleep soundly but when I am at sermon or prayers," says Friar John, and "we begin our morning prayers with coughing, and supper with drinking."

But Rabelais was no Protestant reformer; he gave only tepid approval to Luther, and he mocked Calvin as "the mad devil . . . the impostor of Geneva." Ridiculing the religious certainties of the day, he defined God as "that intellectual sphere the center of which is everywhere and the circumference nowhere." Yet time and again he stated his belief in the basic principles of Christianity, and he remained a Catholic until he died.

The tales of Gargantua and Pantagruel illustrate the confrontation of humanistic scholarship with medieval ways and customs. On the one hand the tales are an indictment of social evils, on the other hand they indicate a rollicking acceptance of man as he is. All Rabelais' ideas are cloaked in bawdiness and buffoonery, with no restraints on hyperbole or invective. Every aspect of life was for him an object of laughter.

Because the book was obscene and satirized monks and their ways it was immediately condemned by the University of Paris, and Parlement forbade its sale. That did not prevent France (including Francis I and some of the clergy) from reading it; all five volumes circulated widely.

Rabelais did not philosophize as such; he did not argue or defend opinions; he only presented men and women, good and evil, as he found them, and made them all the objects of mirth. He could be scornful, but only of sham and lying. Like Erasmus, he rejected the Protestants because of their contentiousness, their condemnation of free will and their disregard for the intellect. "Free men," he wrote, "well born, well educated, conversant in honest company, have by nature an . . . impulse which always pushes them to do the good and to withdraw from vice." This was the antithesis of the reformers' view, which was that man was essentially sinful. Rabelais' solutions for the evils of the time were education and *joie de vivre.*

The works of Rabelais are a boisterous and confusing array of the ideas current in 16th Century France. In striking contrast to his work is that of his countryman Montaigne, a gentler man who like Rabelais drew on the classics, but whose writings are marked by calm and order.

Montaigne was born Michel Eyquem, in 1533, of a recently ennobled family. His father, Pierre Eyquem, Sieur de Montaigne, was a Catholic and mayor of Bordeaux, his mother a descendant of Spanish Marranos. From his babyhood Michel was taught by a German tutor who knew no French and who was bidden by the father to speak only Latin to the child. He was later to say, "I was over six before I understood any more French . . . than Arabic," and not until he went to school did he consort with boys of his own age. These two facts were to leave their marks on him the rest of his life.

As a young man he embarked on a career in government and served for a time as court counselor and magistrate of Bordeaux. But Montaigne was a man of contemplation rather than one of action; he shunned controversy and shrank from what he called "the slavery of . . . public duties." In 1571, at the age of 38, he withdrew to his château in Bordeaux and devoted most of the rest of his life to solitary reading and writing. There in a study where he claimed to have 1,000 books, and where the ceiling was carved with Greek and Latin inscriptions—among them Terence's "I am a man; I consider nothing human foreign to me"—he pondered the meaning of life and invented the essay, which was to become one of the most fashionable genres of Western literature.

"THIS SWEET ANCESTRAL RETREAT" *Montaigne called his quiet castle on a Bordeaux hilltop, where he retired to seek peace and detachment. Here, despite civil war and marauding neighbors, he wrote his philosophical "Essays."*

The essay, from the French word *essayer*, to attempt, was a descriptive piece that might deal with any topic from a subjective point of view. The essays were attempts to probe humanity as Montaigne saw it, and they were intensely personal. Of them he said, "I speak to paper as I do to the first person I meet."

The essay was short; it might ramble but it did not sprawl, and it was neither argumentative nor critical. Like Rabelais, Montaigne accepted the world as it was, but whereas Rabelais wrote in a spirit of bawdy merriment, Montaigne wrote in one of contemplation, and sometimes melancholy. Yet pleasure was the chief aim of man, he believed —though reason must keep him from enslavement to nature—and death ought not to be feared.

Like Rabelais, Montaigne looked with skepticism on the religious certainties of the day. He believed that the laws of conscience proceed from custom, not from God, and that whatever men are accustomed to believe they hold to be incontrovertible. But "nothing is certain but uncertainty," he said, and "nothing seems true that may not seem false."

It was largely because of ideas like this that the Reformation could not take hold in France. Montaigne, too, remained a Catholic throughout the turmoil of the Reformation, and thousands were influenced by him and by other French intellectuals who wrote with humanistic optimism about man.

Almost as engrossing as religion in the 16th Century was the subject of political power, and men of all persuasions grappled with its principles. The first to develop a theory of statecraft was Niccolò Machiavelli, a diplomat who turned to writing after an arrested career in government.

Machiavelli was born in Florence in 1469, of an old Tuscan family. He served for 13 years as Secretary to the Chancery of Florence, helping to shape policy at home and traveling on missions to the King of France, the Pope and the Emperor

Maximilian. The government he served was overthrown in 1512, and Machiavelli was exiled by the new rulers.

In bitter disillusionment, he then lived a lonely and frugal life in the country, where his only solace was his books. "When evening comes," he wrote, "I . . . go into my study. Before I enter I take off my rough mud-stained country dress. I put on my royal and curial robes and thus fittingly attired I enter into the assembly of men of old times. . . . I dare to talk with them, and ask them the reason for their actions. Of their kindness they answer me. . . . From these notes I have composed a little work, *The Prince.*"

The Prince was a dissertation on political rationalism in which Machiavelli set forth the thesis that practical politics is divorced from ethics. Machiavelli believed that all men are governed by self-interest; that they are ungrateful, inconstant, false and avaricious; and that the ruler, to be effective, must appeal to these motives.

The Prince therefore glorified the qualities of the lion and the fox, of force and slyness. A prince, Machiavelli said, "cannot observe all those things which are considered good in men, being often obliged, in order to maintain the state, to act against faith, against charity, against humanity and against religion. And, therefore, he must have a mind disposed to adapt itself according to the wind, and as the variations of fortune dictate, and [must if necessary] be able to do evil."

This was a novel assertion at the time, for men reared on the works of St. Augustine and St. Thomas Aquinas had since the Middle Ages linked governing and ethics together. Philosophers almost universally condemned the book for its bitter cynicism and its appeal to dissimulation, but rulers grasped at it. Charles V, Catherine de' Medici, Henry III and Henry IV, and William of Orange all possessed the book and probably studied it; and

even Queen Elizabeth practiced its principles. The book was read all over Europe, and within 75 years the word "Machiavellian" had entered the speech of Italy, England, France and Spain. Elizabethan dramatists, while professing to loathe Machiavellian principles, were fascinated by them. One of Shakespeare's characters, Richard of Gloucester, boasts villainously in *Henry VI (Part III)* that he can "change shapes with Proteus for advantages/And set the murderous Machiavel to school." And Elizabethan audiences hooted and applauded when the tavern keeper asked in *The Merry Wives of Windsor,* "Am I subtle? Am I a Machiavel?"

If Machiavelli gave political theory a name for evil, a more trusting man gave it a name for idealism. That was Sir Thomas More, the English statesman whom Henry VIII beheaded for his refusal to take the King's Oath of Supremacy. For both Machiavelli and More the end of the state was the well-being of its citizens, but More believed that reasonable men could build a just society without having recourse to the amoral expediency of Machiavelli.

More was distressed by the upheaval of his time and its effects on both the state and the Church, and like Erasmus, he was kind but caustic, urbane but devout, and blessed with a gift for whimsy.

His book *Utopia* purports to be a conversation between himself and an imaginary traveler, Raphael Hythlodaeus, who had visited the New World. Traveling into the wilderness Hythlodaeus had discovered the marvelous land of Utopia (from the Greek for "no place"), where men lived in peace and harmony, with a pervading sense of brotherhood and without the corruption of gold or private property; where all were educated; where everyone worked and no one idled; where justice was designed to end the vice, not to destroy the criminal.

Through the character Hythlodaeus (whose name means "skilled in nonsense") More offered a biting

UTOPIA, *Thomas More's mythical island of peace and harmony, is depicted in a map from the 1518 edition of More's fanciful critique. Signs on garlands identify its capital, Amaurote (center), and the source and mouth of its river, Anyder.*

satire of the ills of European society. The inhabitants of the New World were depicted as living in a state of primeval, natural virtue—a virtue that had been corrupted in European civilization. The idea of the noble savage, which was to take revolutionary effect more than 200 years later, was not remote from Thomas More's idea. For the form of the Utopian state More was indebted to Plato's *Republic;* for the conversation with Hythlodaeus, to Plato's *Dialogues;* and for the setting, to the published correspondence of Amerigo Vespucci. Vespucci was the Italian navigator who charted the New World and gave it his name; his account of his voyage was widely read and did much to pique Europeans' interest in the Western Hemisphere.

No country of that era benefited more from foreign adventure than did Spain, whose lead in exploration yielded literature as well as wealth. The descriptions by conquistadors of the exotic lands and strange new civilizations they had found prompted the nation's scholars to write historical accounts of the American conquest. Still other Spaniards wrote histories of Spain and scientific treatises, in a spirit of remarkable detachment, and that attitude carried over into the theater and narrative fiction, bringing on a Golden Age of literature that was to influence all the rest of Europe. A Spanish playwright was the first to apply to the stage the ideas of the romance ballad, thus helping to found drama that glorified the nation. Another Spaniard was among the first to focus on the everyday affairs and the hopes and fears of the common people (as opposed to the deeds of kings and national heroes), thus laying the groundwork for the modern novel.

The most brilliant star in a whole galaxy of great writers was Miguel de Cervantes Saavedra. Cervantes, son of an impoverished surgeon, had an uncommonly checkered career that included work as steward to a prelate in Rome; military service

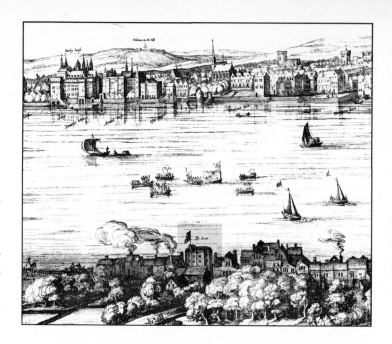

under a duke of Austria, from which he emerged wounded and maimed; slavery in Moslem Algiers; and imprisonment for debt in Spain.

He was one of the few men of letters of his time who was not formally educated in the classics; he was known to his contemporaries as *el ingenio lego*, "the lay genius." He was, however, familiar with the popular courtly romances that had entertained the literate since medieval times.

After his release from Algerian captivity and his return to Spain, Cervantes tried writing, but success was slow to come. He wanted to write drama, but he could not earn a living at it. So he took a job as purchasing agent for the navy, in which capacity he provided some of the stores for the ill-fated Armada when it sailed against England. After being arrested for irregularities in his accounts, he was sent to jail, and there, when he was nearly 60, he began what he fancied would be a short story satirizing the popular chivalric romances. When he was done, Cervantes had written one of the most famous novels in all literature, *Don Quixote*.

Don Quixote is a self-styled knight-errant who sets forth with his servant, Sancho Panza, to battle dragons and evil men, to right injustice, to defend the oppressed and protect the innocent—and he makes a grand nuisance of himself by rescuing beautiful ladies from circumstances they do not wish to be liberated from and by tilting with innocent bystanders whom he takes to be mischievous knights. He dreams of an ideal past, when there was no greed, when all was love and friendship in the world, when "those two fatal words, *thine* and *mine*, were distinctions unknown."

The book is a vast panorama of human society, and the master and his servant are the antitheses of human character: the one courtly and blissfully foolish, the other unlettered but wise; the one trying valiantly to be brave and unselfish in a world that does not live by those ideals, the other shrug-

LONDON'S SWAN THEATER, *largest of the Elizabethan playhouses, stood beyond the city limits on the disreputable south bank of the Thames (top). According to a visiting Dutchman who sketched its circular interior (bottom), 3,000 spectators could squeeze into the Swan's galleries and the pit around its stage.*

ging off the absurdities of life with worldly wise peasant proverbs.

Cervantes had been beset all his life by tribulations, yet his spirit survived unbowed. He could plumb the human soul without Machiavellian bitterness, and be compassionate without being sentimental. He dignified the human spirit even as he made fun of its plight, and he made heroism out of man's aspirations in the face of harsh reality.

Don Quixote was an immediate success in Spain and abroad—it was quickly pirated and translated into all the major languages of Europe—and Cervantes found himself so much in demand by both patrons and publishers that he was able to devote the rest of his life to writing.

By that time Spain's Golden Age was waning. She had lost her grip on the Netherlands, and the ships of her famous navy had suffered a crippling defeat when Philip II, in a historic miscalculation, moved his Armada against England. Spain gave up her supremacy on the seas and lost a part of her foothold in the New World; in a century she began also to lose her distinction in arts and letters.

In England, on the other hand, the defeat of the Spanish Armada swelled an already bursting national pride. While Spain declined, England awoke to a millennium of letters.

Nearly three quarters of a century had passed since Thomas More and his circle had graced English scholarship with classical learning. By this time England had achieved a finer synthesis of the classical with the new than had been accomplished anywhere else. More than a Renaissance, it was a birth of native and original culture.

Like the Italian Renaissance that seeded it, Elizabethan literature celebrated individual man, but it also celebrated the nation-state. Edmund Spenser, a diplomatic aide whose service to the government of England in Ireland won him a castle and 3,000 acres of land in Cork, wrote *The Faerie Queene* as a stately national allegory dedicated to "the most High, Mightie and Magnificent Empresse" Elizabeth. Dozens of other poets and dramatists—John Skelton, Sir Thomas Wyatt, Sir Walter Raleigh, Sir Philip Sidney, Christopher Marlowe—joined in a proud chorus of nationalism and enthusiasm for humankind. Out of their ranks came the man who is the greatest writer in the English language, and perhaps the greatest in any—William Shakespeare.

Shakespeare was born in 1564, the son of a prosperous businessman in Stratford-on-Avon. At some time in his youth he left Stratford for London, where he took a menial job in the theater. Soon he was acting small parts. By 1591, when he was not yet 30, he was writing plays, and a year later one of the popular playwrights of the day warned his colleagues that they were being threatened in the London theater by "an upstart Crow, beautified with our feathers, that with his Tygers hart wrapt in a Players hyde supposes he is as well able to bombast out a blanke verse as the best of you; and being an absolute *Johannes fac totum* [Jack-of-all-trades], is in his own conceit the only Shake-scene in a countrey."

It would be an injustice to Shakespeare to limit him to his time, for the works of this singular genius transcend time and place; even in his era Ben Jonson perceived that he was "not of an age, but for all time." Nevertheless, he was conditioned by the milieu in which he emerged, and he echoes the diverse ideas of that era: the enthusiasm for man, the soaring national pride, the material affluence, excitement over the classics.

Hamlet voices Renaissance exuberance when he says, "What a piece of work is a man! How noble in reason! how infinite in faculties! . . . in apprehension how like a god!" So does Miranda in *The Tempest* when she exclaims, "How beauteous mankind is! O brave new world,/ That hath such people in't!"

Even the ideas that characterized the Reformation got a few nods of acknowledgment. Shakespeare's King John (though he makes no mention of Magna Carta) voices words that might have been uttered three centuries after his time by Henry VIII, when he declares that "no Italian priest/ Shall tithe or toll in our dominions."

The concern with Scripture, and the endless discussion about what truth was to be discerned therein, is parodied in *Hamlet* by the two clowning gravediggers.

> First Clown: ... *There is no ancient gentlemen but gardeners, ditchers, and grave-makers. They hold up Adam's profession.*
> Second Clown: *Was he a gentleman?*
> First: *'A was the first that ever bore arms.*
> Second: *Why, he had none.*
> First: *What, art a heathen? How dost thou understand the Scripture? The Scripture says Adam digged. Could he dig without arms?*

And nationalism is celebrated in the many references to England—

> ... *this scepter'd isle,*
> *This earth of majesty, this seat of Mars,*
> *This other Eden, demi-Paradise,*
> *This fortress built by Nature for herself*
> *Against infection and the hand of war.*

The growing secularism and concern with man on earth, which had already been made manifest in the realm of politics, had its literary culmination in Elizabethan drama, when the passions, energies and ambitions of men enamored of life supplanted concern with the hereafter. There continued to be a struggle between good and evil—a struggle that filled men's hearts with terror—but now it reflected more the vainglory of life than damnation in the hereafter. Medieval men had always looked backward, to a lost Eden that could be regained only when earthly life was ended; curiosity about the material world was subordinated to concern with a world to come. The reformers had looked backward, too, for the restoration of purity in religion; but in bringing attention to man's moral behavior they had brought the focus closer to the present. Now, in the dawn of the 17th Century, men were filled with a yearning for knowledge. They sat up to watch the spectacle of life, which had suddenly turned into an unpredictable suspense drama. This was behind the Elizabethan fascination with the stage.

Like so many cultural revolutions, that of the 16th Century ended by burying the very tools that had set it in motion. An acquaintance with Greek and a re-examination of Latin had brought it about; in the end the classical languages were overtaken by the vernaculars. In 1482, one year before the birth of Luther, the Greek scholar Argyropoulos of Constantinople remarked with satisfaction that "Greece has crossed the Alps." Hardly more than a century later, Ben Jonson praised Shakespeare as "soul of the age ... though thou hadst small Latin and less Greek."

The age had begun with Luther's simple directness; it culminated in Shakespeare's psychological discernment. It had begun with polemics in learned Latin; it culminated in the rise of the modern vernacular literatures. One of Luther's major innovations had been a denial of clerical privileges and an assertion of the priesthood of all believers. Much the same transfer of privilege had come about in literature. When the Reformation era ended, letters were no longer limited to scholars; they had gone out to the people.

ON THE PRODUCTION LINE, *printers set type (left) while an apprentice (center) stacks printed sheets. The man at rear inks type at a second press.*

THE BIRTH OF PRINTING

Some 75 years before the start of the Reformation, the swift dissemination of Protestant ideas—and knowledge in general—was assured by the development of a radical process for duplicating written matter. Around 1440, an efficient method of printing with movable lead type was perfected, probably by Johann Gutenberg of Mainz. He set individual letters in lines and coated them with an oil-based ink, then used a screw-and-lever press to print them, a sheet at a time, on rag paper.

Gutenberg had developed the first genuine mass-production industry—but it was far more than that. Printing grew from fledgling to giant with amazing speed, and with revolutionary results. Presses multiplied in every major city, and more books were printed in a few decades than had been copied by hand in several centuries past. As production soared, plummeting prices put these books within reach of millions. Education—and the means to form one's own opinions—had ceased to be the exclusive property of the clergy and the very rich.

Precious Books Made with Knife and Pen

Before the dawn of modern printing, the making of a book was a slow, expensive process that had improved but little in a thousand years. The professional scribe might spend four or five months copying out a 200-page text; even more costly than his labors were the 25 sheepskins needed to make enough parchment for a book of that length. To be sure, cheaper books were produced by artisans who carved whole pages of words and pictures on single wood blocks, then printed them on paper, most probably using hand pressure. The block, however, printed only its own unchangeable text, and made poor, uneven impressions of words. Though block books could be produced in greater quantity than manuscripts, they did not meet the demand for long, inexpensive texts.

A WOODCARVER, *following his pen-drawn outlines, cuts a block into text and pictures. The chief products of block printing were picture Bibles and playing cards.*

AN ILLUMINATOR *adds decorations to a hand-copied book. The money for 30 such volumes might pay one man's expenses for seven years in 15th Century Italy.*

AN ORNATE LETTER "L," *decorating a hand-copied French Bible, shows an angel staying the hand of Abraham as he prepares to sacrifice his son Isaac to the Lord.*

AN ELABORATE PRINT *was made from a single wood block for a Bible used to teach the illiterate poor. The scenes depict the Esau story (left), the temptation of Christ (middle), and Adam and Eve.*

CASTING TYPE, *a founder pours melted lead into a mold. In the basket below him are finished letters.*

Early Typography

The technological breakthrough that made printing feasible was Gutenberg's method of manufacturing separate letters out of durable metal, to close tolerances. This foundry process, traced in the diagrams at right, produced lead-alloy type quickly and economically, in the huge volume required by printers. For each size of type, more than 150 different characters had to be made—small letters and capitals, numerals, punctuation and ligatures (connected letters such as "ff"). Often 50,000 assorted pieces of type were in use simultaneously on a single job.

At first, type faces were deliberately designed in imitation of hand lettering. Gutenberg's Bible was printed in a heavy, jagged Gothic face that copied 15th Century German penmanship. But as the humanists of the Italian Renaissance rediscovered the forms of classical antiquity, they made and popularized new type faces modeled after the gracefully curved, more readable letters of the Romans. By the early 1600s, the roman letter had triumphed almost everywhere except in Germany; and the basic styles of modern type faces were in widespread use.

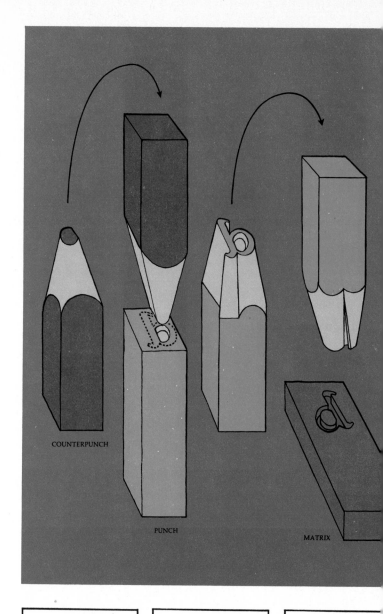

COUNTERPUNCH

PUNCH

MATRIX

FOUR TYPE SPECIMENS *reveal the early trend toward lighter, more refined type faces. They are, from left, Gutenberg's Gothic "black letter" type of 1454; a transitional half-roman, half-Gothic type; the first true roman-letter type of about 1470; and an italic face dating from about 1520.*

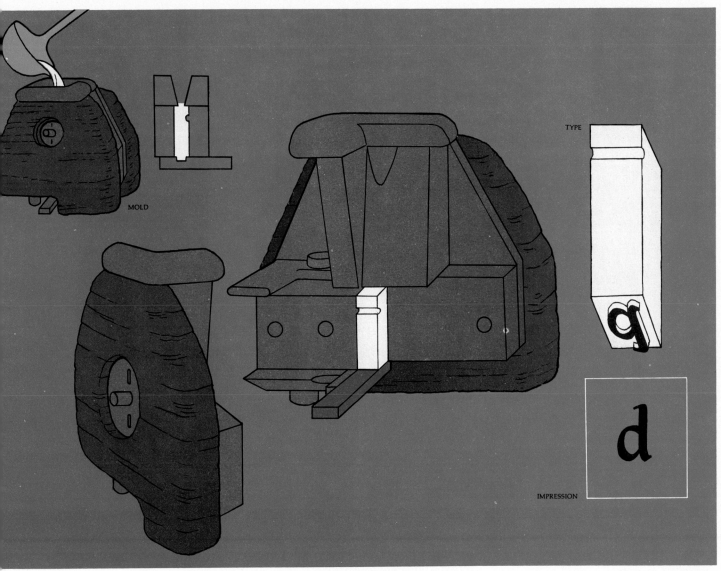

TYPE

MOLD

IMPRESSION

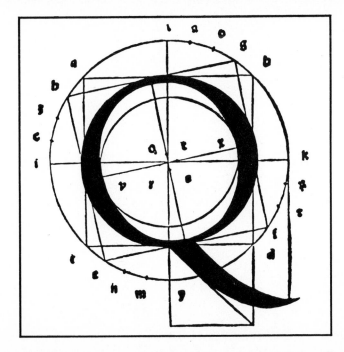

a

*qua fata ſina
ogeniem ſed
dierat, Tyr*

THE MAKING OF A LETTER *involved a sequence of steps. First a counterpunch (blue) was used to indent the closed area, or "counter," of a letter (in this case, "d"), shown in reverse on top of the iron punch. After the letter had been formed by filing away the edges, the punch was hardened and used to make an impression in the soft brass of a matrix (tan). The matrix was then slid into a mold, as shown in the side view and cross section at center. The mold was filled with molten lead, which took on a reverse impression of the matrix and formed the type (white). This printed the letter "d," above.*

A ROMAN CAPITAL "Q," *from a 1514 book on letter design, shows the geometric guidelines used to construct it. Such painstaking work reflected a desire to perfect letter forms.*

A Press and a Process
That Served for Three Centuries

The basic printing press made ingenious use of common devices and techniques. Gutenberg adopted and improved the screw-and-lever presses used in making paper and wine. He developed apparatus to align paper and type precisely and to prevent slippage and ink-smudging while printing. A difficult problem—making uniform impressions with type of varying heights and papers of varying thicknesses—was solved by printing on dampened sheets with pressure enough to force the type into the surface. The common press that developed from Gutenberg's proved so versatile and reliable that it served without major improvements until the cylinder press was invented over 350 years later.

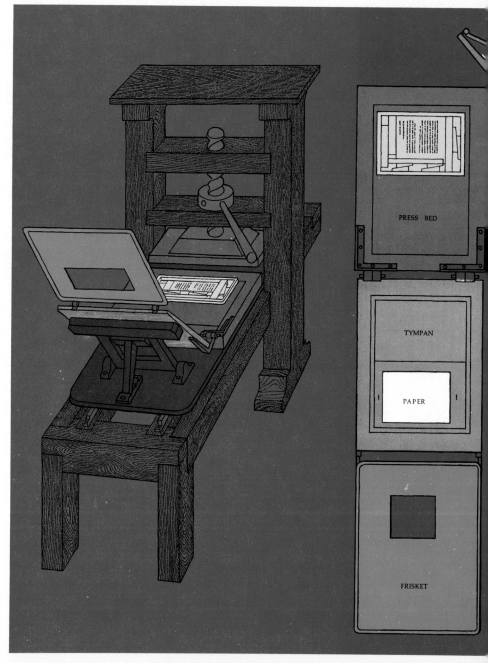

PRESS BED

TYMPAN

PAPER

FRISKET

THE PRINTING PROCESS is illustrated here on a basic early press. The unique part of the printing press was a hinged unit consisting of the press bed (shown throughout in tan), the tympan (red) and the frisket (blue). This assemblage appears in the open position on the press immediately at right; next to this it is shown from above, extended. In preparation for printing, a sheet of paper was placed securely on the tympan, a stretched parchment supported by a frame; the composed type was wedged securely in the bed and then inked with leather-covered pads (seen at upper right). Another framed piece of parchment called the frisket, with a rectangular hole cut out of it to match the type areas, was then folded over the tympan and paper, and both parts were folded over the bed. The frisket, sandwiched in the middle, protected the margins of the paper from ink smears but exposed the type to the paper through its cut-out rectangle. The folded assemblage was then slid into the position shown at far right, directly under the press's screw mechanism. By cranking the long lever, the printer lowered the screw until its flat wood surface pressed the paper against the type, making the ink impression. The total process of printing one sheet on one side took early printers about two minutes.

PREPARING A PRESS, one printer (right) inks the composed type while one of his fellow workers removes a printed sheet of paper. In the background two men work at compartmentalized cases used to store the many kinds of type.

INKING PAD

AN ELEGANT PAGE *from a Gutenberg Bible, issued around 1455, combines the printer's art with an artist's decoration. As the use of such hand-done details declined, the illuminators of Paris in 1511 vainly sued the printers for loss of work.*

The Far-reaching Triumphs of "Divine Art"

The early products of the printing industry were a threefold success—as merchandise, as propaganda weapons and as works of art. Many books rivaled the beauty of manuscript volumes, incorporating handsome design, fine press work and, occasionally, superb illuminations. Less elaborate items sold out as fast as they came from the presses. Luther's German Bible ran through 430 editions in his lifetime. His tracts, and others attacking him, were snapped up at a few cents each. Though Catholic clerics were steady losers in the battle of the printed word, they lauded the new process as "a divine art."

Neapolis

Neapolis vrbs vetusta atqz pclara Campaniæ colum parthenope dicta. Cui origine Tit' lui? Iocta vno refert :. cumais bis verbis. Palepolis fuit haud paul, vbi nic Neapolis e duab' vrbib' fecm ppliæs habitabat cumis erat oriudi. palepolim qd teneret greci dicat infra lui? a publio Clau tio cosule capta fuisse. z infra Ias publ? inter palepolim neapolimqz loco opportune capto diremeras ho stibus societate aureliq munit. Quid3 tn senbui eæ regia cuuate z byomede rege in lattorib' maris codit3 fuisse. Que posthz romanis se sbiecat:eisdæ alisqz piancipib' z vnis fidæ semp seruauit. Liun' q3 dicat Tica polim auxilio nolanoqz romanis tedit fuisse. Tici vero sui semp postea Neapolitani erga romanoqz alios bños costassima fixe. piimu romana republica cinensi clate costern ta ci ad bierione iam byome impen dente cosisterent bello neapolitaniz legati rom somenent ab bis paragata pabere aurei magni poseris in cu ram relate. Qo quide senat' cora more sui accept. z neapolitanis gras egit. Cuqz b anib al Neapoli sum mopqz potiri aseri: Neapolitani in romanoz pnb' pfitcruit. Elozuit aui semp postmodu neapolitana vrbs romana re sub cosulib'. z pariter sub pincipib' integra adeo vt apud eã graues vin animoqz a curiis laxamæ tum quereret. Et discoli Iasicuæ diuersioni. Suetoni' ze nerone reuersus z greca neapolin. qz in ea piimi arte musicæ pnilerat. albis equis meroit bifecta pie murã. Sed z vno videm' iste celeraton. Eirgilius ban. Tmi iuui aliqi. z byorachi Neapoli moratos fuisse. Et Seru' aseri virgaliu scripsisse Georgica nes polg qd parthenopæ appellauit: Franelc? q3 petrarcha pietanti vir ingenio. a Roberto rege neapolitano gallicano onido pgenic rogar? Neapolim bis se conuilit. Sed a trecetis annis citra regia dignitate insigni ta. babet nic neapolita basilicas. menia z arces z publicas z piuatas edes supbas. z ceteris italie ma tonb' coparadas. In qo piæclaris virginis clare mostæni. qd a sancta fir agone regina Robert regia inclit vgore edificani. facile oia italie mostæni antecellit. Eug. piimu esse videat sanen fir atri ceraorbis mari Carusiscæ cenobii codrici magnificena pulcherrimi. Costat ti arcæ mul. Castellis nouis appellatus mari immunens Elpbou regis laude z memoria digniu op'. Ceteris q3 i italia nic crtsit veterib' siue nouis opuo' monumetis z structunis pferendi eæ. Su turru qi' muroruqz altitudine z crassitudine z pulchritudi nem. fiue aularu cubilicqz z singulani es' parcui amplitudine z ornamecta perit' cuusmodi rerus extimet. Visinui' q3 mons cápanie. ab oia alio more solur': Neapoli z qz z q3 q3 mor mila paisui q'nm' eu minet oliue tis z quibusdá fructnieris arbonb' refert'. Es spectris vini vbertate admirabil. qd iam greci vocal. Eru ctauit qziqz cinereus inceda in forma pumiccani arenani. Ira yt et illis campe visqz ad arbozz cacumia intu muerunt. Etzzibus Traiani impzatonis plunu scdue ex vessanensi classe cui pera ad visendu hoc specta culum propiuo acceceret ab incendio absorptus est.

A WALLED TOWN *is shown in a 1493 copy of a German chronicle.*

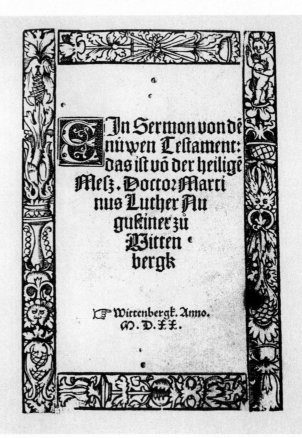

A TITLE PAGE *printed in 1520 announces a Biblical sermon by Luther.*

POLIPHILO QVIVI NARRA, CHE GLI PAR VE AN-
CORA DI DORMIRE, ET ALTRONDE IN SOMNO
RITROVARSE IN VNA CONVALLE, LAQVALE NEL
FINE ERA SER ATA DE VNA MIR ABILE CLAVSVRA
CVM VNA PORTENTOSA PYRAMIDE, DE ADMI-
RATIONE DIGNA, ET VNO EXCELSO OBELISCO DE
SOPR A. LAQVALE CVM DILIGENTIA ET PIACERE
SVBTILMENTE LA CONSIDEROE.

A SPAVENTEVOLE SILVA, ET CONSTI-
pato Nemore euaso, & gli primi altri lochi per el dolce
somno che se hauea per le fesse & prosternate mébre dif
fuso relicti, me ritrouai di nouo in uno piu delectabile
sito assai piu che el præcedente. Elquale non era de mon
ti horridi, & crepidinose rupe intorniato, ñe falcato di
strumosi iugi. Ma compositamente de grate montagniole di non tro-
po altecia. Siluose di giouani quercioli, di roburi, fraxini & Carpi-
ni, & di frondosi Esculi, & Ilice, & di teneri Coryli, & di Alni, & di Ti-
lie, & di Opio, & de infructuosi Oleastri, disposti secondo laspecto di
gli arboriferi Colli. Et giu al piano erano grate siluule di altri siluatici

A SLEEPING FIGURE *illustrates a work printed in 1499 by Manutius.*

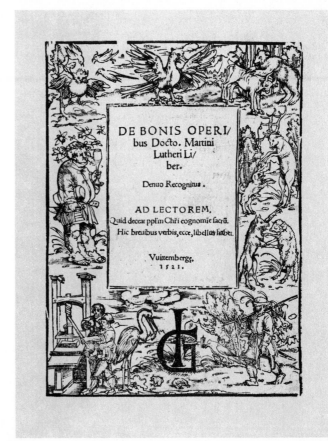

DE BONIS OPERI/
bus Docto. Martini
Lutheri Li/
ber.

Denuo Recognitus.

AD LECTOREM.
Quid decear ppl'm Chri cognomie sacrū.
Hic breuibus verbis, ecce, libellus habet.

Vuittemberge.
1521.

A LUTHER TRACT, *dated 1521, shows a printer at work (bottom left).*

7

LEAN DAYS FOR ART

In almost every age man has devised an art to express the quintessence of his ideals, and more often than not these ideals have been bound up in his definition of God and his pursuit of religious truths. The Egyptians built great pyramids to provide eternal homes for the pharaohs, the rulers they held to be gods incarnate. The Greeks carved statues of their gods in mortal guise, expressing their belief that the gods shared their traits with man. Medieval Christians raised soaring cathedrals to symbolize the awe in which they held their Deity and the Church they believed He had founded on earth.

Yet the Reformation—an era that expended more energy than perhaps any other in history on defining God and expounding religious truth—produced very little in the way of art, and what it did produce said as much of the pride of man as it did of worship of God. Why?

At the time the Reformation began, northern art was far behind that of Renaissance Italy, where a heritage of ancient Greece and Rome and two centuries of affluence had produced an art unexcelled in the history of man. Building on techniques learned from their ancestors, and fired with an imagination that saw life in terms of ideals, Italian painters had produced art that strove to achieve illusion and that sought to convey what man and his world could be at their best. They studied mathematics to learn about perspective, and they studied anatomy to learn how the human body was formed. Having mastered these techniques, they then tried to render on canvas and in marble an idealized nature, with the aim of achieving beauty through harmony.

At the end of the 15th Century, prior to the beginning of the Reformation, art in the north was beginning to move forward as part of the general post-medieval awakening; northern artists were looking to Italy to learn techniques of proportion, perspective, color, and light and shading. But the northern imagination was different from the southern; it had a disposition for detail rather than generality. That proclivity had made the northerners first in mechanics—in mining the earth, devising clocks, and inventing the printing press. It had made them scrutinize the doctrines of faith, take

PLAYING WITH PERSPECTIVE, *which they picked up from Italian Renaissance masters, northern European artists sometimes produced such grotesque exercises as those shown here. They were drawn for a manual on geometry and perspective by Lorenz Stoer, a Nuremberg engraver who was obviously fascinated with scrollwork, Roman ruins and abstract balancing acts.*

the Bible literally, and overthrow a Church that paid no heed to the disparities between its ideals and reality. That same proclivity marked the northern Europeans' art: it made them wish to mirror nature rather than idealize it.

When they learned from Italy the techniques of perspective and lighting, northern artists went on to depict with native scrupulousness the pile of fur, the softness of velvet, the sheen of silk, the delicacy of lace, the glitter of gold, the luster of gems —even facial wrinkles and blemishes, which in an earlier age had been reserved to convey grotesquerie or villainy. Northern artists of the 16th Century accepted these as marks of character and individuality. Whereas the Italians had sought to depict in art the sublimity that the human being was capable of attaining, the northerners, who believed that man was essentially sinful, showed how nature had run away with the divine intention.

The absorption of southern techniques into northern art made its first appearance in the person of Albrecht Dürer. Like others of his time, Dürer—who lived in the time of Luther, but who did most of his work before the Reformation had rent the Christian world asunder—possessed a religious view of life. It was a view that saw the world as a battleground between God and the devil, and man as prey to forces beyond his control. His early works show terrifying visions of Doomsday —a heritage of the Middle Ages, when men were beset with fears of a world they did not understand. But Dürer studied in Italy. He was not the first northern artist to do so, but he was the first to put Italian knowledge to a use that would carry northern art beyond the limitations of Gothic images. Drawing on scenes from classic mythology, stories from the Bible and others from German daily life, and blending Italian symmetry with northern detail, he rendered an art that ridiculed the follies of man and pondered over his fate.

Dürer was born in 1471, the third child of a family of 18 and the son of an accomplished goldsmith in Nuremberg. As a child, he was apprenticed to his father's trade, but he showed such a talent for drawing that his father moved the boy from his own workshop to that of the most famous woodcut artist in the city. When he had outgrown this he went to learn copper engraving at Colmar, a town in Alsace that had a vigorous printing industry. Next he went to Basel, where he worked at book illustrations, and then to Italy, where he acquired a knowledge of anatomy. Finally, having mastered painting, woodcutting and engraving, he returned to Nuremberg to open his own shop.

Dürer saw himself as a missionary who would bring about the reform of northern art. He pondered diligently over the beauty of Italian painting and how it was achieved; he performed many experiments, painting figures that were now elongated, now widened, in an effort to find the perfect form. He kept diaries of his travels and wrote prodigiously on his view of art, that others might have the benefit of his knowledge. Though he employed the techniques of perspective and proportion that he had learned in Italy, he retained his northern attitude, and this shows both in his drawings and in his writing. The Italian painter Raphael, imbued with the southern quest for the ideal, wrote, "To paint a beauty, I need to see many beauties." Dürer, in contrast, declared that "the more exact and like a man a picture is, the better the work. . . . Others are of another opinion and speak of how a man should be . . . but in such things I consider nature the master and human imaginations errors." He believed until he died that there must be a secret geometrical formula to account for the beauty of the Italian nude.

Still, Dürer represented much of the spirit of examination and questioning that characterized the

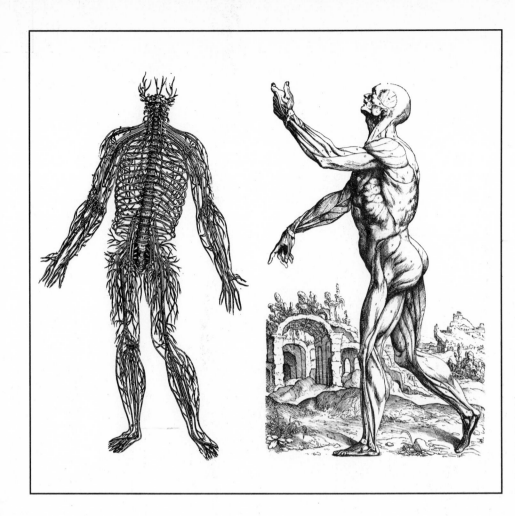

THE HUMAN ANATOMY *was first accurately analyzed in Italy by Andreas Vesalius in his monumental work, "De Humani Corporis Fabrica." Published in 1543, it influenced not only physicians but artists in northern Europe. Painters and sculptors gained invaluable knowledge from detailed studies such as those at left, which Vesalius and artists hired by him made from dissected cadavers.*

early 16th Century. He continued to draw pious subjects, because piety was still very much a part of the era, and because Zwingli and Calvin had not yet linked imagery with idolatry, but the piety of his drawings was the piety of the common people, a piety for which he translated the life of Christ into the life of the German people and for which he set the scene in the familiar German countryside. To these subjects he added others expressing his observations on the follies of man. One of his most famous works is an engraving entitled *Melancholia I*, in which a woman with wings too small for her body sits gloomily in the midst of the symbols of man's accomplishments—a compass, a book, a balance, a hammer. The picture represents man's aspirations, but instead of glorifying these, as an Italian humanist might have done, Dürer mocks the vanity of human knowledge —symbolizing the northern deprecation of the intellect in favor of faith.

At first Dürer had to bargain, like any artisan, to sell his works—promising to use only the best paint and plenty of it. But as his fame spread he was engaged as court painter by the Emperor Maximilian. When at the age of 50 he visited the Netherlands, he was honored in Antwerp with a formal banquet at the guild hall; "and when I was led to the table," he wrote, "the people stood, on both sides, as if they were introducing a great lord, and among them were many persons of great excellence who all bowed their heads in the most humble manner." This marked a shift in the social standards of the north; it was not long since the artist had been looked down upon for laboring with his hands.

Although he faithfully mirrored the great forces that gave his era their character, Dürer remained a Catholic. Other artists, too, found it possible to see —and portray—all viewpoints in the religious conflict that swirled about them. They were employed for propaganda purposes by both sides, and most of them would work for either so long as it paid.

Perhaps the most notable example of a painter who prospered from the patronage of Protestants and Catholics alike was Lucas Cranach. Cranach (who took his name from Kronach, the town where he was born, in 1472, and where he was trained in painting in his father's shop) was a Lutheran. His were the pictures of Luther that appeared all over Worms at the time of the reformer's trial. He also painted or engraved pictures of virtually every German personage who played a part in the Reformation, illustrated Luther's first New Testament, and served as court painter to three successive Electors of Saxony. But Cranach was no fanatical partisan of reform. He also painted Crucifixions and Madonnas for Catholic clients, and some of the woodcuts from Luther's Bible were used in a Catholic edition.

Cranach was no mere laboring hand; he was a versatile entrepreneur. He ran a workshop with a host of well-trained assistants who turned out much of the work that bears his name. Like most painters in that age, he belonged to the apothecaries' guild (compounding paints was considered not much different from mixing medicines); but unlike the others, Cranach actually practiced the apothecary's trade. He ran a printing works, a bookshop and a paper mill. He also sat on the town council of Wittenberg and twice served as mayor. He was one of Wittenberg's wealthiest citizens; he lived in luxury and was courted by all the great men of Germany—even the Emperor Charles V. When Charles, in one of his efforts to halt the tide of Protestantism, went to war againt the Schmalkaldic League, he marched into Saxony in 1547; yet he overlooked Cranach's consorting with the heretics and summoned the painter to his camp for an interview.

Cranach—aided by his assistants—was one of the

INNOCENCE AND PIETY, *deftly captured in this chalk sketch by the German master Hans Holbein, shine forth in the features of a burgomaster's young daughter, Anna Meyer. Holbein later worked Anna's profile into a painting for an altarpiece.*

most prolific painters of the era. A record in the electoral accounts for 1533 indicates that in that year alone he was paid for "60 pairs of small paintings of the late Electors." His tombstone bears the epitaph *pictor celerrimus*, "swiftest of painters." His fame was almost his ruin, however. He began his career promisingly, but with success he turned slick and careless. He exercised scarcely any influence on German art; his taste and his techniques were thoroughly Gothic, and therefore behind the times. He drew elaborate clothes, but he ignored the principles of anatomy and his faces were plain; they conveyed only the features of the subject, and nothing of the character that resided behind them. While he lived he was a dominant figure in Germany—but that was owing more to the patronage of Frederick the Wise and the friendship of Luther than to his talent.

The growing importance of characterization—and, thus, of the secular man—is most apparent in the work of Hans Holbein the Younger. Holbein was born about 1497 in Augsburg, Germany, to a large family whose members were already distinguished masters of painting in that region. He learned almost from birth the best of both northern and Italian techniques.

In 1514 Hans and his brother went to Basel, where Hans was engaged by the printer Froben to illustrate several books, among them More's *Utopia* and Erasmus' *Praise of Folly*. Soon he was designing altarpieces, painting portraits of the local bourgeoisie, and decorating the walls of private houses and the town hall.

In less than a decade, however, art was beginning to take a turn for the worse. Zwingli had by this time established himself in Zurich, and with his spreading influence the demand for religious art in Switzerland petered out and art in general became suspect; indeed, Erasmus wrote, "The arts here are freezing." Bearing this statement in a letter of

introduction to several of Erasmus' friends, among them Sir Thomas More, Holbein went to seek his fortune in England.

One of his first jobs there was a group portrait of More and his family. Partly through his initial introductions from Erasmus, partly through his growing acquaintance with More, he won rapid acceptance among the nobility, and before long he was appointed official court painter to Henry VIII. As such he designed costumes, jewelry, goblets, table silver, furniture and other castle appointments, and weapons. He painted the walls and ceilings of the palace chambers. He designed the King's state robes, down to the jewel-studded buttons and shoe buckles; he also designed the robes and jewels that Henry presented to his several wives. But Holbein's main job was to do portraits of the royal household. Windsor Castle today displays 87 of his drawings, and among them are pictures of the men who played the major roles in Henry's reign.

In his early work Holbein used his skill with detail to adorn the background of his characters. He placed each subject in a setting natural to his calling—a merchant, for example, at a table laden with coins and papers; an archbishop accompanied by his miter, a crucifix and the Bible; an astronomer with a compass and quadrant. As he grew older and his skill matured, Holbein dispensed with these details to concentrate on the subject alone, and in doing this he achieved a mastery of character portrayal that has never been surpassed.

Holbein was not only a craftsman who could combine the techniques of northern detail with southern perspective and color more successfully than anyone else ever had; he possessed a poet's grasp of the human soul and a philosopher's detachment. His portrait of Sir Thomas More caught the melancholy strength of the man who was later to lay down his life for his faith. His many paintings of Henry VIII portray the masterful King in all his arrogance—yet despite their frankness, these pictures do not seem to have incurred the displeasure of the royal egotist.

Perhaps Holbein's greatest achievements are his portraits of Erasmus. These are among the most eloquent portraits ever painted, and the most humanistic—eloquent because they convey both the philosopher's absorption in study and the sorrows he suffered in his last years; and humanistic because they show the nobility of the man's character.

With Holbein's death in 1543, the art of the north came to a standstill. The Reformation stifled it—partly because of the energy expended on religious quarrels, partly because of the emphasis on austerity. Some portrait painting continued to be done, but it turned mannered and artificial. Only in the Netherlands would art survive the Reformation; when that country recovered from its protracted struggle against Spain, it would emerge in the 17th Century as the undisputed leader of northern art. By then, however, the era was no longer that of the Reformation.

The influence of Catholicism on 16th Century art was somewhat more positive than that of the Reformation, though it imposed restrictions of its own. The Church did not condemn art, as Calvinist churches did, nor ignore it, as did the Lutheran churches. But in the attempt to meet the charges of immorality that had arisen out of the Church's involvement with the Italian Renaissance, the Council of Trent took stern measures restricting the painting of nude bodies, and put all Church painting under strict regulation. Pope Pius V ordered the figures of the Michelangelo frescoes in the Sistine Chapel partially clothed (unfortunately, by a second-rate artist) and removed the pagan statues from the Vatican.

The Council of Trent did, however, affirm the validity of sacred paintings and sculpture, believing that images could inspire and even instruct the unlettered faithful. The emphasis, however, was now on reinforcing the doctrines that had been attacked by the Protestants.

In Spain, the center of the earliest and most vigorous Catholic reform, art thrived under the patronage of the Church and Philip II; here it reflected the grave religious soul of the Spaniard and the propagandizing of the Church in defense of the challenged faith.

The best known of the many artists who worked in Spain during Philip's reign was not a Spaniard at all; he was Domenico Teotocopulo, called El Greco because he came from the Greek island of Crete. In 1577, after working some years in Venice under the influence of Titian and Tintoretto, El Greco left Italy for Spain—possibly indignant at having had his work criticized for being "incorrect." He was to remain in Spain for nearly 40 years, until his death, and there he developed a style that was a marked departure from anything that had been done before him. He was no ascetic —he was widely hailed and well rewarded during his lifetime, and he lived in opulence—but he seems to have shared, or readily adopted, the Spaniards' mysticism. In any event, he vividly conveyed its mood with a skillful use of light and somber shading, and with figures that are long, thin, slightly distorted and unearthly, reminiscent of the Byzantine art that prevailed in his native Greece.

After the time of El Greco, art in Catholic countries moved in the direction of the baroque. As the Church went on the defensive and papal demands for supremacy grew more insistent, churches and tombs became ornate and pretentious. (The secular monarchs of the following century, who were to claim supremacy themselves, were also to adopt the baroque style in secular art.) Classic simplicity was lost, and art became a medium of propaganda, designed to impress by pomp and grandeur rather than by subtlety. Quality gave way to cheap-

AN ORNAMENTAL LETTER S, *part of an alphabet designed by Theodor de Bry, illustrated a 16th Century German religious text. Wreathed in a profusion of heavenly and earthly symbols, it shows the high skill of Reformation engravers.*

ness—marble to plaster and gold to tinsel. The concerted attempt to reach the unlettered led to an increased emphasis on emotional impact and dogmatic orthodoxy.

The work of Dürer, Holbein and El Greco can match the art of any era, but these men were exceptions to the general rule of the age. Apart from them and a few others (notably in Italy), neither the Protestants nor the Catholics of the Reformation produced much art of note.

The leaders of both faiths did, however, avail themselves of one new medium of expression in the battle they waged from the third decade of the century onward. The invention of printing had made possible mechanical reproduction of images, just as it did of words. Dürer, Cranach and Holbein were all expert at making woodcuts and copper engravings for illustrating books and pamphlets, and Cranach in particular did much work as a Lutheran propagandist. Besides his Bible illustrations and the posters at Worms, Cranach portrayed Luther preaching and "working in the vineyard of the Lord" and engaging in other activities that would advertise the Lutheran cause. These were widely circulated. Pamphlets and leaflets caricaturing the Pope and lesser antagonists of Luther also had great popularity, and were answered in kind from the Catholic side. These were the predecessors of latter-day newspaper cartoons.

Architecture declined all over Europe except in France, where, in place of churches, there were erected bigger and more elaborate domestic dwellings. It was in the 16th Century that the Louvre in Paris (originally built as a royal fort in the 13th Century) and Fontainebleau (built in the 12th) were enlarged and acquired most of the characteristics they have today, and that many of the great chateaux of the Loire Valley were constructed. The early chateaux, those at Blois and Chambord, are predominantly Gothic, but as the 16th Century wore on, Italian influences became more and more pronounced. King Francis I, who had warred with Charles V and the papacy on Italian soil, brought back Italian artists to design and decorate his palaces, and Italian statues and paintings to adorn them. Under his son, Henry II, the same artists commissioned by Francis continued to work on the Louvre and Fontainebleau.

Tours, Caen, Toulouse, Bourges, Rouen and other cities all have châteaux built by the affluent civil servants at the court of Francis. Francis' tax collector in Normandy built Chenonceaux, which Henry II later appropriated to make a gift to his mistress, Diane de Poitiers (and which Catherine de' Medici took from Diane after Henry's death). In all these buildings Italian Renaissance influence is apparent—the arches begin to be less pointed and more rounded, the façades are embellished with classical columns and the interiors with classical friezes.

Crafts and minor arts meanwhile flourished all over Europe to an extent unsurpassed in any preceding civilization. The ceramics of China, enamels of Persia, rugs of Turkey, perfumes of Arabia, metal work of Damascus and silks of India inspired European emulation. Gold, ivory, spices, fine furs, precious stones and pearls had to be imported; but they were in constant supply, especially once exploration increased the traffic with foreign ports. Fine textiles, table appointments, edged tools and leather goods had become commodities available to all who could pay for them, and they adorned the houses that, with the passing of feudal warfare, had ceased to be fortresses and acquired ever more domestic comforts. Never and nowhere had there been such a profusion of industries, such a multiplicity of products, or such distribution of wealth to support a broad market. There was poverty indeed, but wealth that once was the privilege of nobility had now become available to a prospering bourgeoisie; and the bourgeoisie was growing ever larger.

It was this great middle class that patronized the art of the Reformation. It was in many respects a limited art, but despite that, the turmoil and the changing social conditions of the era can be traced in it. In medieval times the artist had been an anonymous craftsman who rendered in images the ideals shared by all in Christendom. His patron was the Church, and his audience was all the faithful who worshiped. With the coming of the Reformation and the shattering of old traditions, ideals were no longer held in common. As the turmoil of the 16th Century splintered religion and society, it dissipated artistic energy. The artist, the patron, the subject matter and even the audience underwent metamorphosis, and when they did, art was diverted from the religious to the secular.

The secularism of Reformation Europe was not the deliberate pursuit of worldly pleasure that marked the Renaissance in Italy—indeed, men of the Reformation scorned any preoccupation with worldly pleasure as sinful. Secularism in the north was a phenomenon that came in stealthily. Just as the state took charge of the Church, so living men eclipsed the saints; scenes from daily life superseded those of religion, and the dwelling replaced the house of worship as the object of adornment. The artist found his patron in the king, the prince or the burgher, his subject in the world around him, and his audience in the man who could pay to buy his art. The artist himself was now a professional who signed the picture he painted and gave his name to the architectural plans he devised.

All of these developments arose out of the same principle that underlay the re-examination of God and the Church: the rising importance of man and his place in the world. Out of the same principle was born the idea of progress, and progress was to be the driving force of the centuries that lay ahead.

A SPIRAL STAIRCASE, *built by Francis I for his château at Blois, displays lavish Renaissance details.*

A NEW STYLE FOR CHANGING TIMES

By 1500 the intellectual ferment in northern Europe that was to produce a religious revolution had already created a taste for change in other fields. In architecture, designers and their patrons embraced the bold new style of Italy's Renaissance, using its classical forms first as decoration and later with a surer grasp of structural principles. The so-called "Italian manner" spread steadily northward. French kings applied it in palatial châteaux *(above)* that reflected their growing confidence and power. Dutch burghers used it proudly in fine new homes and civic buildings. German and English noblemen grafted it onto their great houses as a mark of their cultural attainment. Within seven decades, the Italian style had become the international style—and a symbol of the age's secular trend.

INTRICATE PINNACLES *atop the church terminate in crosses or small spheres. Below are other popular Renaissance features: round-headed arches; pilasters, or flat columns; medallions and geometric designs formed by marbles of different colors.*

AN ORNATE WINDOW *in the Certosa's façade epitomizes north Italian opulence. The window is bisected by a graceful centerpiece of candelabrum design. On each side of it is a row of medallions and a pier with classical statues in shell niches.*

A Fantastic Churchfront
That Started a Vogue

Italian Renaissance architecture can almost be said to have been launched on its conquest of northern Europe by a single building. In the 1490s, as the French kings pressed their claim to portions of Italy, their troops occupied the Duchy of Milan. In nearby Pavia the Frenchmen were confronted by the Certosa, an old church which was then being given a new and startling Renaissance façade. This ornate marble facing completely captivated the French, satisfying both their appetite for novelty and a love for flamboyance reflected in their own rich late-Gothic style. Nobleman after nobleman on the way south to the battlefields came to view the façade and marvel at its columned galleries and its carvings of scrolls, shells, cherubs and cornucopias. One Frenchman ecstatically called the Certosa "the finest church I ever saw."

Under royal leadership, French enthusiasm for the Renaissance style took numerous forms. King Charles VIII shipped north from Naples, in one huge consignment of booty, 87,000 pounds of Italian tapestry, books, paintings and sculpture—and brought home with him several Italian artists and craftsmen as well. Francis I, crowned King in 1515, was a passionate devotee of Renaissance style in all things. He imported a host of talented Italian artists and architects, forming a workshop at Fontainebleau. The great sculptor Benvenuto Cellini was lured north by Francis' promise—"I will choke you with gold." The universal genius of the Renaissance, Leonardo da Vinci, spent the last few years of his life as Francis' guest.

After 25 years of futile campaigning, France's armies retreated from Italy in disarray. But even before they abandoned Pavia, its church's decorations had become a fashionable feature in the building plans of every up-to-date French aristocrat.

THE CERTOSA'S INFLUENCE *can be discerned in sketches comparing the church's rooftop decorations (right) with those of Chambord (far right). Details shared by both buildings include numerous pinnacles, round medallions and slender, elaborately decorated pilasters.*

A HYBRID CHATEAU, *Chambord combines a late-medieval façade with an ornate Renaissance roofscape. The highest pinnacle, at center, crowns a double spiral staircase that may have been built to a design by King Francis' aged Italian guest, Leonardo da Vinci.*

A Vast Pleasure Palace for France's King

The Italian style, transplanted first into France's Loire Valley, flowered there in dozens of magnificent châteaux. The most spectacular of these was Chambord, which King Francis I began building in 1519, probably from a plan by an Italian architect. In basic design, this 440-room edifice was a medieval castle with great round towers and long, thick-walled wings. But the new Italian decoration topped Chambord's roof with a fantastic array of shapes—slender pinnacles, carved dormer windows and no less than 365 ornate chimneys. Italian style also lent a new grandeur and worldliness to court life at Chambord. As many as a thousand guests would ride out on a single hunt; and Francis himself, attesting to a different kind of sportive pastime, scribbled on a chamber wall, "Woman is fickle."

WINDOW TREATMENTS *in the Certosa church (left) and in Heidelberg Castle (right) reveal similarities in rectangular proportions, in the use of friezes, moldings and pediments above, and in niches with sculptured figures at the sides.*

A Princely Monument
on a Grand Germanic Scale

Around 1550, the Italian style entered Germany by way of France and the Netherlands. Its heralds were books on architecture by Renaissance writers, as well as paintings and popular prints by northern artists who had studied in Italy, among them Albrecht Dürer. Their stylistic message soon became the rage. Italian decoration was applied in elaborate overlays to the high-gabled, many-windowed buildings of Germany's late-Gothic period and built into many new castles and guildhalls.

Italian style reached its German zenith in Heidelberg Castle, a great complex of interconnected buildings ranged around a huge court. One wing, named the Otto Heinrichsbau after the prince who built it, was both monumental in scale and profuse in ornamentation. Sculptors completed the building in a lavish—and eclectic—manner. The interior façade alone, shown at right, displayed classical statues representing three Old Testament personages, five Christian virtues and eight Roman and Greek gods.

AN ELABORATE FAÇADE, *framed by an archway leading into Heidelberg's courtyard, uses powerful decorative lines to break up its*

enormous expanse. Horizontally, heavy moldings mark the level of the building's three floors, and stone crosspieces bisect the tall win- dows. Vertically, each pair of windows is separated by high niches containing statues and is flanked by pilasters made of rough stone.

A Growing Sense of Structure

For more than four decades, northern enthusiasts of the Italian style happily troweled it on as pure decoration. But gradually they came to learn, chiefly from the skilled architects of Rome, the underlying structural principles that went back to the classic architecture of the Romans and the Greeks. In expressing these principles, they produced stronger, more graceful Renaissance buildings, whose every detail was fused into a harmonious whole. For example, logical systems of columns—no longer merely decorative—supported or seemed to support the heavy friezes and pediments. In such structures, the northern Renaissance style finally came of age.

A FUNCTIONAL THEME—*the use of paired columns to support an arched opening—is seen here in Renaissance structures built in three countries in the late 16th Century. Ruins of a French building near Aix-en-Provence (left) include a triumphal arch reminiscent of its ancient Roman models. The same motif, extended and repeated vertically, looms over Antwerp's town hall (above) and appears over the entrance to England's Burghley House (right).*

A Flowering of Native Style

North of Paris, between a wide moat and a spired chapel, stands a building that suggests the final triumph of Italian Renaissance architecture—its development into various national styles. The Petit Château of Chantilly was built for the

Montmorency family around 1560. By then France and other countries no longer had to rely solely on Italian architects. Chantilly's designer, Jean Bullant, was both a Frenchman and a trained professional, and he gave ample evidence of his skill and taste in the château's elegant proportions and subdued decoration. He also added themes of northern origin, such as the dormer windows rising in a rhythmic row along the roof. The final product was distinctively, and picturesquely, French.

Knappn

8

THE POWER
OF PROTESTANTISM

SILVER MINING *in Saxony is celebrated in a 16th Century altar painting by Hans Hesse. Commissioned by miners for St. Anne's Church in Annaberg, it reflects not only the growing importance of precious metals in Europe's new money economy, but also an increasing respect for the dignity of work.*

The Reformation was the threshold of the modern age. In 1500, the Europe of Luther's youth was still essentially medieval—accustomed to the supranational and paternalistic roles of the Catholic Church and the Holy Roman Empire, inhibited in its attitude toward the natural world, unsophisticated in its primarily agrarian economy and unaware of the lands lying to the west. One hundred and fifty years later the world had a new look. The Americas had been settled, Protestantism had taken over a good share of Rome's domain, Europe's political geography had taken on much the shape it has today, a scientific revolution was underway, and capitalism had become a dynamic economic principle.

Of course these changes did not occur all at once. The first stage of the religious revolution ended with the Council of Trent in 1563; the Reformation's effect on the political map of Europe was not really clear until the end of the Thirty Years' War in 1648. In the interim, the various currents of the Reformation swirled along in a heady, often explosive, mixture that overturned the old ways and produced some startling effects in the process. One of the most unfortunate of these was a violent obsession with witchcraft, which stands out as one of the most grisly signposts of the age.

Witches had long been a familiar part of the European landscape. It was accepted as a matter beyond question that Satan was everywhere, and that some humans, succumbing to his blandishments, sold their souls to him. Satan's end of this fateful bargain (which of course denied salvation to the humans) was to give the newly recruited witches certain powers that enabled them to influence the weather and do mischief to their fellow men. Such misfortunes as a brewer's beer spoiling, a farmer's crops failing, babies crying continually or wives falling in love with the wrong husbands were clear evidence that witches were doing the devil's work. It was understood that witches met occasionally at an obscene Witches' Sabbath, where they worshiped Satan (disguised as a goat or other animal) and celebrated orgiastic rites with his henchmen, the lesser devils.

Even otherwise skeptical 15th Century humanists

accepted the existence of witches, but it took the religious zeal of the 16th Century to turn witch-hunting into the frenzied hysteria that it became during the 16th and 17th Centuries. Pope Innocent VIII set a precedent in 1484 with a papal bull inspired by the Scriptural injunction, "Thou shalt not suffer a witch to live." Other Churchmen followed this a few years later with an infamous text called *Malleus Maleficarum* ("The Witches' Hammer"), which described how to recognize witches and how to punish them. As the increased spiritual awareness of the Reformation brought a corresponding sensitivity to the ever-present powers of Satan, the mania increased and any misfortune—a tree struck by lightning, a calf born dead—set off a search for a witch. Neighbor distrusted neighbor, and no one was safe from suspicion.

At the height of the mania, to be charged with witchcraft was tantamount to conviction, for the magistrates generally considered any defense or denial by the accused to be the work of the devil and proof of complicity. Confession was required for conviction, however, and torture, as prescribed in the *Malleus Maleficarum*, was the key to confession. Tortures were varied and cruelly imaginative. In England weights were piled on the victim's chest until the witch confessed or died. Other effective means of persuasion included sticking pins under the fingernails, thrusting the feet into a fire and stretching the body on the rack.

A confessed witch would sometimes escape with a whipping, but the usual sentence was death by burning. On the day of execution the witch was led or dragged to a great stake raised in a public place and piled about with wood. While the luckless victim burned, great crowds gathered to watch with vociferous approval. Fortunate indeed were the accused who were strangled to death before the fire was lit.

The craze raged over most of Europe for nearly

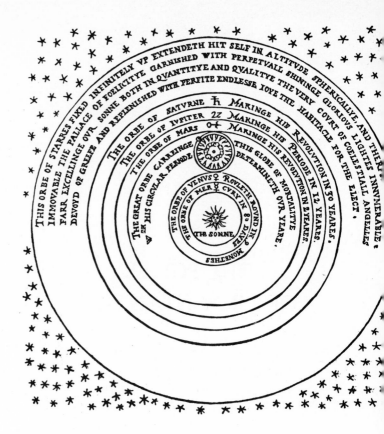

200 years. In Spain and Italy, where the Inquisition functioned, witchcraft was treated as a form of heresy, and Inquisitors sometimes spared penitent witches from the death sentence. Elsewhere, however, witch-hunting was the job of the secular authorities, and leniency was discouraged as a dangerous weakness. The prevailing attitude was expressed by Jean Bodin, an eminent French jurist who wrote: "Whatever punishment one can order against witches by roasting and cooking them over a slow fire is not really very much and not as bad as the torment which Satan has . . . prepared for them in hell, for the fire here cannot last more than an hour or so until the witches have died."

The total number of men, women and children put to death as witches during the period from 1500 to 1700 can only be estimated, but certain figures are available. It was recorded that in Calvin's Geneva, for instance, 34 witches were executed in 1545. But that was trivial compared with the record in Germany, where the flame of witch-hunting burned most cruelly. In five years the Bishop of

OPERNICUS' UNIVERSE, *neatly diagramed by the English mathe-*
atician Leonard Digges, revolutionized traditional astronomy
enthroning the sun, not the earth, at the center of the cosmos.

Bamberg is said to have burned 600 witches. A cautious estimate puts the number of witches killed in all of Germany during the witch-hunting craze at 10,000, but some historians have figured the total as high as 100,000.

The zealous war against witches was part of the cloud of superstition that hung over a society in which the average citizen still believed firmly in ghosts, omens and spells. But a tiny minority of thinkers in the 16th Century, affected by Renaissance curiosity, quietly examined the world they could actually see and touch. Although the 16th Century scientists were themselves still heavily burdened with superstition and handicapped by their devotion to ancient authorities, they nevertheless contributed to the observation and classification of natural phenomena that provided the starting place for the brilliant scientific innovators of the following century.

In the study of anatomy, for example, the work of Andreas Vesalius was instrumental in righting errors that had persisted for 14 centuries—ever since the Greek physician Galen set forth his medical theories in the Second Century A.D. So great was the influence of Galen's teaching that anatomists prior to the time of Vesalius had ignored experimental evidence that disagreed with the ancient sage. Vesalius, on the other hand, performed hundreds of anatomical experiments and rejected Galen wherever he found a conflict. At 23 Vesalius was a professor in Padua (he later became physician to Charles V and to his son, King Philip II of Spain), and in 1543 he published the first known complete textbook of anatomy, *De Humani Corporis Fabrica* ("On the Fabric of the Human Body"), a beautifully illustrated treatise which still ranks as an outstanding work in its field.

A more colorful if not more productive contemporary of Vesalius' was a Swiss healer with the resounding name of Philippus Aureolus Theo-

phrastus Bombastus von Hohenheim, who called himself Paracelsus, a made-up name that suggested he was superior to the great Roman physician Celsus. Paracelsus recognized no peer in medicine, ancient or modern, and he is said to have demonstrated his conviction in 1527 by publicly burning the works of Galen in Basel.

Despite his flamboyance, Paracelsus made many valuable contributions in the field of chemical medicine, using mercury and antimony in the treatment of disease. He also made the first careful clinical study of the diseases that plagued miners.

Almost every science showed similar progress. Gerhardus Mercator devised a way of drawing a flat chart of the earth's curved surface that was more accurate than any previous method. Mercator's projection is still a standard cartographic technique. The nature of magnetism was explored; Leonardo da Vinci made important discoveries about the physics of acceleration and momentum; the Swiss zoologist Conrad Gesner wrote the *History of Animals*, a comprehensive text that served until the 19th Century.

Even the calendar was revised, under the prodding of Pope Gregory XIII, to correct the errors of the Julian calendar, which had been in use since the reign of Julius Caesar. The old calendar gave a few too many minutes to the year, and by the 16th Century the cumulative error had put the calendar at odds with the natural yearly cycle by a full 10 days. On the basis of astronomers' calculations the modern Gregorian calendar was devised; in 1582 Gregory ordered that in all Catholic countries October 4 would be followed by October 15; ten days were "lost" and man was back on schedule with the seasons again. (Protestant countries, in their antagonism to the Pope, strenuously resisted the Gregorian calendar; England did not accept it until 1752.)

The era of the Reformation recorded one brilliant

achievement in science that matched any of the next ages to come. Just before his death, in 1543, the Polish astronomer Nicholas Copernicus published *On the Revolution of the Celestial Orbs*, in which he denied that the earth is the stationary center of the universe; instead, he asserted, the earth revolves on its axis and moves, with the other planets, around the sun. At last the concept of an earth-centered universe, proposed by Ptolemy in the Second Century and accepted by all thinking men ever since, was challenged by a man who, though short on empirical proof, had the mathematical genius and clarity of thought to make a great intellectual leap. Copernicus' theory had many faults and it had little impact on his immediate contemporaries. But it struck a spark in the murky mists of medieval astronomy and furnished a light that guided the great astronomers of the next age, like Galileo and Kepler, along the path toward scientific truth.

The scientific promise of the 16th Century had to wait for another age to be fully realized, but other changes swept Reformation Europe so rapidly as to make their effects quickly apparent. Some of the most important of these were in the field of economics. The 16th Century witnessed a spectacular rise of capitalism, which was to become a dominant economic principle of later centuries.

Many factors combined to bring this about. One of the most basic was an increase in population. Figures are far from exact, but from 1450 to 1600 Europe's population probably increased by about 17 million, or almost one third. This surge may have been due partly to improved living conditions and partly to changed social conditions that made it easier for men to establish themselves and marry younger. Whatever the cause, more people meant a bigger market and a larger labor force, two prerequisites for economic expansion.

The second development basic to the economic revolution of the time was the sudden expansion of Europe's horizons. As the intrepid explorers of Portugal and Spain opened new routes to the East and discovered new lands in the West, new imports and wealth began flooding European markets. The valuable Asian spices that had previously arrived by caravan via the Near East now traveled around the Cape of Good Hope by sea, and the centers of trade shifted from the Mediterranean to the Atlantic ports. In the year 1503 alone, four years after Da Gama's first voyage around Africa to India, Portugal imported 1,300 tons of black pepper. A year later the price of spices in Lisbon had dropped to a fifth of that in Venice, and the Venetian monopoly on the spice trade was broken forever.

Perhaps the most important cargo carried by the ships of the 16th Century was the silver and gold that flowed in prodigious amounts from the mines of the Spanish New World to the ports of Cádiz and Seville. Spain poured the bullion into the rest of Europe in exchange for the guns, food and supplies it needed to execute its grandiose imperial schemes. Suddenly there was more money in Europe than there had ever been before. One effect of the influx was a gradual, century-long inflation that set off a price revolution throughout Europe. By 1650 the amount of precious metal in Europe had tripled, and so had prices. Wages did not keep up with the cost of living, so inflation hurt the wage earner as well as landowning aristocrats whose rents were fixed by custom. The winners in this economic transformation were the merchants and entrepreneurs, who dealt in goods and money. And as they prospered, so did capitalism.

Capitalism was by no means new to Europe. In late-medieval times, cities such as Venice, Genoa and Bruges had been centers of capitalistic enterprise. But that capitalism had been limited by the provincial nature of trade, by the Church's condemnation of usury and by the generally cumbersome business methods of the Middle Ages. Now, with the flood of liquid capital in the 16th Century came more sophisticated banking practices that made possible the use of credit on a large scale. Furthermore, growing trade led to increased production in such industries as shipbuilding, textiles, arms and armor. All of these required large amounts of money, which shrewd capitalists were ready to supply, for a profit. In the Middle Ages, money had been regarded as sterile, valuable only as a medium of exchange; now the capitalistic practice of using money to make money became more and more widespread.

Not all the factors contributing to the success of capitalism were secular. In the vigorous, new spiritual force of John Calvin's Protestantism there was much that was congenial to the thriving new economic attitude. The Calvinists believed that a citizen demonstrated his fitness for salvation by being law-abiding, industrious, sober and thrifty. These same virtues served so well to help the rising bourgeois capitalist on his path that many historians have suggested that Calvinism was one of the main sources of the capitalistic spirit. Other scholars disagree, pointing out that capitalism thrived also in Catholic countries. (The most powerful financiers of the day, the Fuggers of Augsburg, were devoutly Catholic.)

There is no doubt, however, that capitalism and Calvinism were admirably suited to each other. The development of Puritanism, a variation on the Calvinist habit of thought and way of life, furnishes a clear example of the propitious compatibility of the new enterprising spirit with the Protestant religion.

The Puritans—whose name was originally a term of derision, given them for their excessive scrupulousness—arose in England in the 1560s. They were a group of radical nonconformists who believed that the Elizabethan Reformation had retained too many Catholic ways and wished to purify the Church of England of "popishness," by which they meant episcopal hierarchy and elaborate ceremony.

The Puritans were repressed by Queen Elizabeth, who believed that Calvin and his followers were "overbold with God Almighty, making too many subtle scannings of His blessed will, as lawyers do with human testaments." More important, she deplored the Calvinist practice of lay participation in Church affairs, for she foresaw that a voice in the Church would lead to a voice in the state, and thus threaten the monarchy. James I harassed the Puritans with laws requiring conformity to the Church of England, for like his predecessor, he was determined to retain royal prerogatives as head of the Church and state. It was during his reign that the most radical Puritans, unwilling to compromise with the Church of England and thwarted in efforts to change it, fled to the New World.

But despite the derision of their fellow citizens and in the face of royal measures taken against them, the Puritans were widely influential. More than any other group of reformers they stressed the importance of individual responsibility and duty. In England as on the Continent the commercial class was rising; in both places the Calvinistic emphasis on industry and dedication appealed to the earnest men of the new class. As they made their way into the House of Commons their sober and diligent habit of thought imprinted itself on Englishmen of all classes. The hallmarks of the Puritans—their sturdy characters, the determination with which they toiled and the individual responsibility they encouraged—were to become the backbone of capitalistic enterprise and the inspiration of republican government. These were the same qualities that tamed the American wilderness.

This was still in the future, however. Before the Reformation was settled, one last destructive convulsion lay ahead that was to put a bloody end to the old order and to mark the close of the era. This was the Thirty Years' War. And Germany, which had been the stage for the opening scenes of the

Reformation, was also the stage for its final act.

In 1555 the Peace of Augsburg, by which the Emperor Charles V had granted the princes the right to determine the religion of their subjects, had given recognition to both Lutherans and Catholics, but not to Calvinists. Neither did this settlement silence the vilification that Lutherans and Catholics engaged in. Then the Calvinists began to make significant gains in the 1560s, but in many instances the Protestants were as bitterly contemptuous of one another as were the Catholics and Lutherans. Divided against itself, Germany lay open to the designs of the other nations of Europe.

The Thirty Years' War—begun nominally in the cause of religion, but actually in a struggle for political power—was in one respect a civil war in which German Protestants warred against German Catholics. In another it was a civil war in which German princes of both faiths pitted themselves against their Emperor. In still a third respect it was an international war, in which France challenged the Habsburgs, the Spaniards tried doggedly to recapture their hold on the Dutch, the recently awakened Scandinavians endeavored to cut themselves portions of the Continental pie, and nations standing on the sidelines aided now one combatant, now another, with money, troops and treaties.

In this multifaceted struggle the armies of six peoples fought actively: Germany, Spain, France, Bohemia, Denmark and Sweden. Others—England, Poland, Scotland and Transylvania—provided mercenary troops, and their ranks were filled out with Greeks, Turks, Italians and Dutch. The generals who commanded the troops were frequently avaricious and adventurous opportunists—men who had no convictions of faith, no loyalties of nationality, but who coveted prizes of territory and power.

Underlying this imbroglio was international hatred of the Habsburg Dynasty, whose far-flung family (divided into two branches since 1556,

when the Emperor Charles V bequeathed Spain to his son and the Empire to his brother) controlled lands that bordered on all the nations of Europe.

In 1619 the Habsburg Emperor Ferdinand II was also King of Bohemia. The Bohemian nobles, who were predominantly Lutheran, deposed him as King and in his place elected a young German Protestant Prince. The Emperor, aided by money from the Pope and troops from Spain, sent an army into Bohemia to oust the Prince, reclaim the crown and restore Catholicism; in Germany, Ferdinand stripped the Prince of his rights and property. The King of Denmark, seizing on the resulting disorder in hopes of acquiring new land for his son, came to the aid of the German Prince.

In an effort to re-establish Catholicism in Germany, the Emperor issued the Edict of Restitution, by which the many properties that had been confiscated from the Catholic Church in the years of conflict following 1552 were to be restored to it. The edict met with some resistance, but Imperial troops saw to its enforcement. Now the King of Sweden, offering himself to the Protestants as savior of the faith, marched into Germany and the international conflagration was on.

It might have been expected that Catholic France would go to the aid of the Catholic bloc, but the French had an animosity for the Habsburgs that went back many generations. So the French entered the war—at first secretly, later openly—by providing money to finance the Swedish troops and forming alliances with the Protestant Netherlands and England, and with Catholic Savoy and Venice. And by now the Spanish, who had come to the aid of their Imperial cousins against the Germans, were using German soil as a base from which to attack the Dutch.

Thus the struggle went on for years, with one nation after another entering the fray in Germany. As the religious issue began to diminish and the

A PROTESTANT CRUSADER, *23-year-old Duke Christian of Brunswick was one of many German nobles whose armies spread terror during the Thirty Years' War. He appears here amid 46 Catholic towns and castles he ravaged during campaigns in Hesse and Westphalia.*

struggle for power became more overt, the Germans had a change of heart: the terms Protestant and Catholic lost their dread significance and those of Frenchman, Swede and Spaniard grew more forbidding. The arrival of the Swedish King had at first given the Germans hope and courage, but in time they came to resent the presence of a foreign king and alien troops on their soil. The Emperor, seizing on this development, won the support of Germans of both faiths by offering to withdraw the Edict of Restitution in return for assistance against the Swedes.

This was a momentous development, for it was an assertion of German unity against foreign intervention. Now Catholic and Protestant Germans were allied with a Catholic Emperor against an alliance of Protestant Swedes and Catholic French. And the Habsburgs had in the meantime even turned against their Catholic Spanish cousins, with

whose struggle against the rebelling Dutch they no longer sympathized.

Thus one army after another dragged itself across the soil of Germany for 30 years, killing, raping, burning, sacking, leaving famine and disease in their wake, quartering the troops in the homes of the people, seizing women and children for servants. The population of Germany in that period fell, according to a modest estimate, by as much as a third. By 1640 her cities lay in ruins, her villages were deserted, her fields untilled and her roads torn up. The people had taken to eating dogs and horses, even human corpses. In 1637, when the Emperor died, his son inherited a prostrate and friendless Empire.

By now the Germans were crying for surcease, and the new Emperor began negotiations for an end to the war. A conference finally opened at Westphalia in December 1644, and to it diplomats came from Spain, France, Sweden, Holland, Switzerland, various Italian states and the Vatican. They wrangled for nearly four years. On October 24, 1648, they finally signed the Peace of Westphalia, which settled the religious question. More significant, it redrew the map of Europe and redrafted the concept of international relations.

The treaty renewed the principle of the Peace of Augsburg, by which religion was territorially determined, but added recognition for Calvinism. From that time onward Protestantism and Catholicism were stabilized.

In his immediate domains the Emperor was confirmed in the same right that the princes had in Germany—to determine the religion of his subjects—but the Imperial authority was now limited to Austria, Bohemia and Hungary.

In Germany the princes were granted rights of sovereignty. The Emperor was forbidden to make laws, raise taxes, declare war or negotiate treaties without the consent of the states. The figurehead ruler of the now-decrepit Empire resisted this arrangement, but in vain. With local jealousies thus perpetuated, Germany was to remain in political disorder for two centuries to come.

The Imperial borders split off; the Dutch Republic and the Swiss Confederation were formally recognized. Part of the Rhine's valley went to France, its mouth to the Netherlands; parts of the Baltic regions went to Sweden. Germany, deprived of control of her great waterways, could not regain her former commercial eminence. And with the Habsburgs' domains fragmented, the international pre-eminence of that family was broken.

The delegates who signed this treaty comprised the most massive congregation of European dignitaries since the Council of Constance in 1415. But that gathering had treated affairs of the Church; this one treated affairs of state. Unlike their Constance forebears, who had seen themselves as members of a united Christendom, the diplomats at Westphalia had no bonds in common—religious, political or other; they saw themselves as belonging to sovereign units. That fact and the terms of the treaty they signed are measures of the changes that had come over Europe. When the guns were silenced after the Peace of Westphalia in 1648, the last echoes of Luther's hammer on the Castle Church in Wittenberg died away as well. The Reformation as an era had come to an end.

What had the Reformation wrought, besides bloodshed and vilification? Its founders began with expressions of individualism, but demanded the most rigid conformity of their followers. They challenged the authority of the Roman Church, to replace it with the authority of the Bible. Their followers preached the gospel of love and practiced fratricide.

Notwithstanding, the Reformation had changed the face of Europe. In severing kings and their subjects from Rome, it had contributed to the growth of the modern nation-state. In rebuking the licentiousness of the Renaissance, it had brought virtue and morality back to religion. And despite its demands for conformity, the Reformation could not obscure the fact that its origins lay in individualism; the individualism of its founders would shine as a beacon for future generations.

Neither popes nor kings had been sterner bigots or fiercer tyrants than Luther and Calvin, but rebels must be ruthless to survive. Even so, Luther and Calvin had brought the people into disputes that in earlier ages had been left to scholars and priests; thus they opened the way for democracy, for once men began to voice opinions about religious faith, they moved on to make themselves heard in government as well. Luther with his priesthood of all believers and Calvin with his doctrine of the elect unwittingly contributed to a greater emancipation of man than either of them envisioned.

THE SIMPLE VOCATION *of the shepherd, like other humble jobs, achieved a greater dignity when Luther stressed the equality of all men before God.*

LUTHER'S LEGACY

Martin Luther's views on religion were so widely condemned in his own day that at times even he lost his nerve. Wondering whether he had been presumptuous to defy all of Christendom and centuries of tradition, he once asked himself: "Do you mean to say that all the previous teachers knew nothing . . .? Are you alone the nest egg of the Holy Ghost in these last times?"

Such moments of self-doubt, however, were rare. Two years after the pope had excommunicated him, Luther was writing, "He who does not receive my doctrine cannot be saved," and later he signed his will, "Martin Luther, God's notary." Thousands flocked to his banner in his own time, and today 70 million Lutherans —most of them worshiping in Germany, Scandinavia and the United States— govern their lives by his once revolutionary doctrines. His reforming influence is still felt most strongly in his native Germany, where the daily life of the people and even the stark landscape itself seem to be stamped by his powerful words.

"He who wants to be saved should be so minded as if there were no human being but he alone,
and that the consolation and promise of God through all the Scriptures concerned him only."

The individual, Luther believed, is as alone before the Almighty as a man facing the evening sky—nothing can stand between him and God. Luther said flatly, "The Christian man must examine and judge for himself."

His own spectacular struggles with the Catholic Church often distracted Luther from his solitary confrontation with God. Even while hunting, he imagined that his dogs were "impious magistrates, bishops and theologians." And he could not refrain from comparing his views of nature with those of the Church. "We now look deeper into creation than we did under the papacy," Luther said. "They used to pass it by, looking at nature with the interest of a cow."

*"God our Father has made all things depend
on faith so that whoever has faith
will have everything, and whoever
does not have faith will have nothing."*

Luther believed that man is saved by faith alone. Unlike his Catholic opponents, Luther insisted that good works—such as prayers and pilgrimages—can never redeem sinful man; only through faith in God's love and sympathy can believers hope to lead a truly Christian life and win salvation after death.

Luther's own faith struggled constantly against doubt and superstition. Time and again the devil

tempted him and he would break out in a cold sweat of anxiety—"the devil's bath," he called it. One residence he dubbed a "house of demons," and he found many regions infested with evil spirits ("Prussia is full of them," he said). Encounters with God were even more exhausting. "I dispute much with God with great impatience," he once said. Often he felt God was angry with him and asked: "Why does God pick on me alone?"

"When we begin to have faith, at the same time we begin to die to this world and to live to God in the future life. Thus, faith is verily both death and resurrection."

"Not only are we the freest of kings,
we are also priests forever,
which is far more excellent than
being kings, for as priests
we are worthy to appear before God
to pray for others and
to teach one another divine things."

If faith alone is needed for salvation, Luther argued, "then faith makes all people priests and priestesses, be they young or old, Lords or servants, women or men, scholars or laymen." This principle of "the priesthood of all believers" made each member of the congregation equally important. This contradicted the Catholic view that only ordained priests could grant absolution for sins and only they possessed the miraculous powers needed to perform the Mass. Luther argued instead that priests were only officeholders appointed to conduct church services and to educate and inspire the congregation with sermons.

To Luther's adherents, the arbiter of God's will was no longer the pope, but the Bible. Before the Reformation very few laymen read the Scriptures (Luther himself never saw a complete Bible until he was 20). Now, however, the Word of God was universally available; Luther's translation of the New Testament—still used in Germany today—appeared in 1522. This Bible, with pictures that identified the Antichrist with the pope, became Germany's bestseller; more than 100,000 copies were sold during his life. Luther's hymns and catechisms appeared in churches far and wide; and between 1521 and 1524 more religious pamphlets were published than at any other time in German history. Soon Lutherans claimed that the average churchgoer was better educated in the Bible than many priests had formerly been. The control that the pope once had over the German mind could never be restored.

"A cobbler, a smith, a farmer, each has the work and office of his trade...
and everyone by means of his own work or office
must benefit and serve every other, that in this way many kinds of work
may be done for the bodily and spiritual welfare of the community,
even as all the members of the body serve one another."

The Catholic Church for centuries had divided Christians into clergy and laity, and insisted that the clergy was superior. Luther sharply denied that there was any such division. Just as he declared that all believers were priests, so he preached that all occupations were holy, from the blacksmith at his forge to the potter at his wheel (shown here in modern Germany).

In his own calling as preacher and writer Luther labored with superhuman energy; "If I rest I rust," he once explained. Although racked with colic, kidney stones, ulcers and gout, he wrote so much that his works are only now being published in their entirety. When the definitive German edition is completed, it will include some 130 volumes plus six books of chance remarks he made that his students preserved.

Luther claimed the Bible abounded with examples of hard work. Christ was a carpenter, Mary kept a clean house; even the shepherds, he pointed out, went back to their flocks after seeing the Christ Child. "Surely that must be wrong," Luther quipped. "We should correct the passage to read, 'They went and shaved their heads, fasted, told their rosaries, and put on cowls.' Instead we read, 'The shepherds returned.' Where to? To their sheep. The sheep would have been in a sorry way if they had not."

The most important vocation any man or woman can have, Luther taught, is raising a family. He and his wife Katherine devoted themselves to their own family; besides their own six children they took in 11 orphans. "Married people," Luther said, "should know that they can perform no better and no more useful work for God, Christianity, the world, themselves, and their children, than by bringing up their children well. . . . On the other hand, hell cannot be more easily deserved . . . than by neglecting children, letting them swear, learn shameful words and songs, and do as they please."

"Baptism is water with the Word of God,
and this is the essence and whole substance of baptism.
When, therefore, water and God's Word are conjoined,
it must necessarily be holy and divine water,
for as the Word is, so the water becomes also."

Life is not being religious," Luther said, "but becoming religious." For him, the Church's sacred rites of Baptism and Communion were acts aimed at this goal: "You are continually baptized anew by faith." Similarly, Communion re-enacted the Crucifixion and its promise of God's love—which once caused Luther to wonder if "God can forgive me for having crucified Him with Masses twenty years running."

Today Luther stands primarily as a titanic influence rather than as a systematic thinker. Though he wrote popular declarations of the new faith that are models of clarity, his scholarly attempts to order his theology failed. When his students treated him as an infallible lawmaker, he complained, "They are trying to make me into a fixed star. I am an irregular planet."

"The whole power of the mass consists
in the words of Christ in which he testifies that forgiveness
of sins is bestowed on all those who believe
that his body is given and his blood poured out for them.
Nothing is more important for those who go to hear mass
than to ponder these words diligently and in full faith."

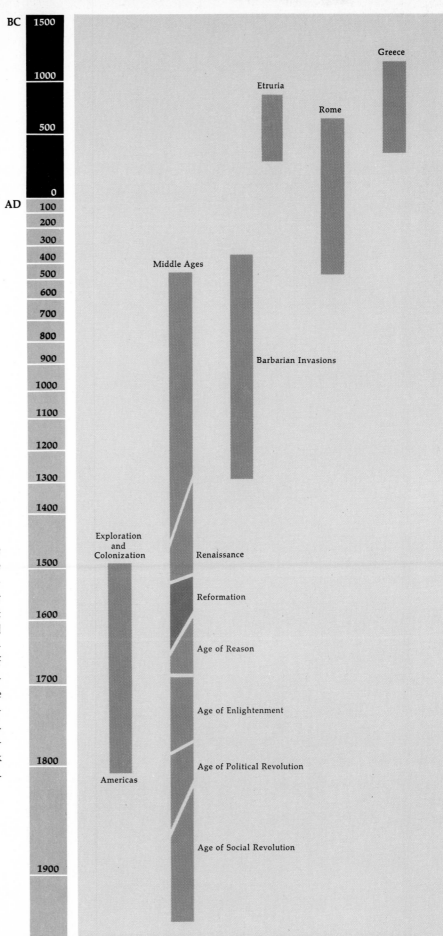

BC

1500

1000

500

0

AD

100

200

300

400

500

600

700

800

900

1000

1100

1200

1300

1400

1500

1600

1700

1800

1900

Greece

Etruria

Rome

Middle Ages

Barbarian Invasions

Exploration
and
Colonization

Renaissance

Reformation

Age of Reason

Age of Enlightenment

Age of Political Revolution

Americas

Age of Social Revolution

GREAT AGES
OF WESTERN
CIVILIZATION

The chart at right is designed to show the
duration of the Reformation, and to relate
it to the other cultural periods of the Western world that are considered in one major
group of volumes of this series. This chart
is excerpted from a comprehensive world
chronology which appears in the introduc-
tory booklet to the series. Comparison of
the chart seen here with the world chronology will enable the reader to relate the
great ages of Western civilization to important cultures in other parts of the world.

On the following pages is a chronolog-
ical listing of important events which took
place during the era covered by this book.

CHRONOLOGY: *A listing of significant events during the Reformation*

Religion and Politics

1483   Martin Luther is born in Eisleben, Saxony

1485   Henry VII begins the reign of the House of Tudor in England

1494   Charles VIII of France invades Italy

1498   Savonarola is burned at the stake in Florence for heresy

1499   Louis XII of France launches a second invasion of Italy, conquers Milan

1505   Martin Luther enters an Augustinian cloister in Erfurt at the age of 22

1509   John Calvin is born; Henry VIII becomes King of England

1510   Luther leaves on a mission to Rome for his monastery

1512   Luther is awarded his doctorate at the University of Wittenberg

1515   Francis I becomes King of France

1516   Under the Concordat of Bologna, Francis I gains the right to nominate French bishops and abbots

1517   Luther posts his 95 Theses on the door of Wittenberg's Castle Church

1519   Luther debates with John Eck in Leipzig; Ulrich Zwingli begins the Reformation in Switzerland; Charles I of Spain is elected Holy Roman Emperor, thereby becoming Charles V

1520   Henry VIII and Francis I meet near Calais on the Field of the Cloth of Gold to arrange an alliance; Luther burns the papal bull condemning him

1521   At the Diet of Worms, Emperor Charles V issues an edict declaring Luther an outlaw; war breaks out between Charles V and Francis I

1522   Franz von Sickingen and Ulrich von Hutten lead the Knights' War against ecclesiastical principalities; Sickingen is killed, Hutten flees Germany

1524   The Peasants' War breaks out in Germany and is suppressed within a year

1525   Francis I is defeated by the forces of Emperor Charles V at Pavia

1527   Second war begins between Charles V and Francis I

1529   Princes supporting Luther protest the Edict of Worms at the Diet of Speyer, become known as "Protestants"

1530   The Lutheran doctrine is set forth by Melanchthon at the Diet of Augsburg

1531   Zwingli is killed in Zurich by the army of the Catholic League

1533   Henry VIII marries Anne Boleyn and is excommunicated by the Pope

1534   With the Act of Supremacy, Henry VIII becomes head of the Church of England

1535   Sir Thomas More is beheaded for opposing Henry's break with Rome

1536   Henry VIII beheads Anne Boleyn, suppresses England's monasteries

1540   Society of Jesus (Jesuits) receives papal approval

1541   John Calvin sets up theocratic government in Geneva

1545   Council of Trent undertakes reform of the Church under Jesuit guidance

Literature, Art and Science

1484   Albrecht Dürer paints his first self-portrait

1488   Munich's Frauenkirche, one of the last great cathedrals, is completed

1494   Sebastian Brant publishes *Ship of Fools*

1499   Erasmus travels to England, meets Thomas More and John Colet

1506   On his second trip to Italy, Dürer paints the *Feast of the Rose Garlands*; German humanist John Reuchlin publishes first Hebrew grammar by a Christian

1507   Martin Waldseemüller publishes Amerigo Vespucci's correspondence, suggests that the New World be named after him

1509   Erasmus writes *The Praise of Folly*

1512   Michelangelo finishes painting the ceiling of the Sistine Chapel

1513   Machiavelli, in retirement, writes *The Prince*

1514   First volume of Cardinal Jiménez' Complutensian Polyglot Bible is completed

1515   *The Letters of Obscure Men*, an anonymous satire, attacks the Church in Germany

1516   Sir Thomas More publishes *Utopia*; Erasmus' New Testament appears

1520   Luther writes the *Address to the Christian Nobility of the German Nation, The Babylonian Captivity of the Church* and *Treatise on Christian Liberty*

1522   Luther's New Testament appears, with woodcuts by Lucas Cranach; Ignatius Loyola writes his *Spiritual Exercises*

1523   Lefèvre d'Etaples publishes the New Testament in French

1525   William Tyndale begins printing of the English New Testament

1527   Paracelsus lectures on his "new medicine" at the University of Basel

1528   Simon Fish publishes the *Supplicacion of Beggars*, an attack on the English clergy

1530   Francis I establishes the Collège de France as a center for humanism

1532   Rabelais begins publishing his comic masterpiece *Gargantua and Pantagruel*

1534   First complete edition of Luther's Bible appears

1535   Hans Holbein the Younger paints *The Ambassadors*

1536   John Calvin publishes *Institutes of the Christian Religion*

1538   Lucas Cranach paints his *Crucifixion*

1539   *The Great Bible* by Miles Coverdale is issued in the name of Henry VIII

1543   Copernicus' *Revolutions of the Celestial Orbs* is printed; Vesalius publishes his *Structure of the Human Body*

1546   Architect Pierre Lescot is commissioned by Francis I to build the new Louvre

1500

1510

1520

1530

1540

1552 French lyric poet Pierre de Ronsard completes his *Amours*
1554 Protestant clergyman John Foxe publishes the *Book of Martyrs*

1556 Agricola writes *De re metallica* on metallurgy and mining
1557 Genevan ministers in Brazil hold the first Protestant service in the New World
1559 Pope Paul IV publishes the first Index of Prohibited Books naming 48 heretical editions of the Bible

1563 Philip II of Spain begins building the Escorial palace
1564 John Knox completes his *History of the Reformation in Scotland*

1568 Pieter Brueghel the Elder paints *The Blind Leading the Blind*
1572 Portuguese poet Luís de Camões publishes his epic work *The Lusiads*

1573 Tycho Brahe publishes *On the New Star*; Lope de Vega writes his first play, *El Verdadero Amante* (The True Lover), at the age of 12
1574 Italian poet Torquato Tasso finishes *Jerusalem Delivered*
1576 French political philosopher Jean Bodin writes *The Republic*
1580 Montaigne publishes his first *Essays* on various forms of government

1582 Pope Gregory XIII commissions calendar reforms
1586 El Greco paints the *Burial of Count Orgaz*

1596 First six books of Edmund Spenser's *The Faerie Queene* appear

1599 Shakespeare becomes a partner in London's new Globe Theatre

1605 Miguel de Cervantes publishes Part I of *Don Quixote*
1607 Claudio Monteverdi's first opera, *Orfeo*, is produced
1609 Johannes Kepler publishes *Astronomica Nova*; Galileo builds his telescope

1611 King James Version of the Bible is printed; Shakespeare's *The Tempest* is performed

1624 Velázquez is made court painter by Philip IV
1625 Hugo Grotius writes *On the Law of War and Peace*, a pioneering text in international law

1628 William Harvey publishes *On the Movement of the Heart and Blood in Animals*
1638 Galileo's *Dialogues Concerning Two New Sciences* appears
1642 Rembrandt paints *The Night Watch*
1644 Milton writes his *Areopagitica*, Descartes his *Principles of Philosophy*

1550 **1560** **1570** **1580** **1590** **1600** **1610** **1620** **1640**

1547 Edward VI becomes King of England; Henry II takes the throne in France
1552 War breaks out between Emperor Charles V and France's Henry II
1554 Queen Mary I of England, a Catholic, marries Philip II of Spain
1555 Restoration of Catholicism in England leads to Protestant persecution; Peace of Augsburg divides Germany between Lutheran and Catholic princes
1556 Emperor Charles V abdicates and retires to a monastery; Ferdinand becomes the Habsburg ruler; Philip II ascends the throne of Spain

1558 Elizabeth is crowned Queen of England, restores Protestantism
1559 Under the Treaty of Cateau-Cambrésis, France abandons her claims in Italy; John Knox leads reform in Scotland
1561 Mary Stuart becomes Queen of Scotland
1562 Religious and civil wars begin in France as Huguenots take arms

1567 Spanish army under the Duke of Alva moves into the Netherlands to suppress revolt
1572 Parisian Protestants are slaughtered in the Massacre of St. Bartholomew

1576 The Netherlands provinces unite under the Pacification of Ghent to drive out the Spaniards

1581 Northern Netherlands provinces proclaim their independence from Spain

1587 Mary Queen of Scots is executed for conspiracy against Elizabeth
1588 The Spanish Armada is routed by the English fleet, aided by strong gales
1589 Henry IV founds the Bourbon dynasty in France

1597 Irish Rebellion against England is led by Hugh O'Neill, Earl of Tyrone
1598 Edict of Nantes gives legal recognition to the Huguenots in France

1603 James I of the House of Stuart is crowned King of England
1604 Guy Fawkes is executed for "Gunpowder Plot" to blow up Parliament

1610 Henry IV is assassinated; his son, Louis XIII, becomes King of France

1618 Protestant German princes and Catholic Habsburgs start the Thirty Years' War

1625 Charles I ascends the throne in England

1642 Civil War between Roundheads and Cavaliers breaks out in England
1643 France's Louis XIV begins his 72-year reign

1648 Peace of Westphalia ends the Thirty Years' War

BIBLIOGRAPHY

These books were selected during the preparation of the volume for their interest and authority, and for their usefulness to readers seeking additional information on specific points. An asterisk (*) marks works available in both hard-cover and paperback editions; a dagger (†) indicates availability only in paperback.

GENERAL READING

†Bainton, Roland H., *The Reformation of the Sixteenth Century.* Beacon Press, 1963.

†Brodrick, James, *The Origin of the Jesuits.* Image Books, 1960.

†Burns, Edward McNall, *The Counter Reformation.* D. Van Nostrand, 1964.

*Burton, Elizabeth, *The Pageant of Elizabethan England.* Charles Scribner's Sons, 1962.

*Daniel-Rops, Henri, *The Catholic Reformation.* Transl. by John Warrington. E. P. Dutton, 1962.

Durant, Will, *The Reformation.* Simon and Schuster, 1957.

†Elton, G. R., *Reformation Europe 1517-1559.* Meridian Books, 1964.

Geyl, Pieter, *The Revolt of the Netherlands.* Barnes and Noble, 1958.

*Gilmore, Myron P., *The World of Humanism 1453-1517.* Harper and Row, 1952.

Grimm, Harold J., *The Reformation Era 1500-1650.* Macmillan, 1954.

†Harbison, E. Harris, *The Age of Reformation.* Cornell University Press, 1962.

Hillerbrand, Hans J., *The Reformation.* Harper and Row, 1964.

Holborn, Hajo, *A History of Modern Germany,* Vol. I, *The Reformation.* Alfred A. Knopf, 1961.

*Hughes, Philip, *The Church in Crisis: A history of the general councils, 325-1870.* Doubleday, 1961.

*Huizinga, Johan, *The Waning of the Middle Ages.* St. Martin's Press.

*Mattingly, Garrett, *The Armada.* Houghton Mifflin, 1959.

†Miller, Perry, and Thomas H. Johnson, eds., *The Puritans.* 2 vols. Harper Torchbooks, 1963.

New Cambridge Modern History, Vol. II, *The Reformation.* Cambridge University Press, 1958.

Parker, T. M., *The English Reformation to 1558.* London, Oxford University Press, 1963.

†Powicke, Sir Maurice, *The Reformation in England.* London, Oxford University Press, 1965.

†Rupp, Gordon, *Luther's Progress to the Diet of Worms.* Harper Torchbooks, 1964.

*Smith, Preserved, *The Age of the Reformation.* Henry Holt, 1947.

Thompson, James Westfall, *Economic and Social History of Europe in the Later Middle Ages (1300-1530).* Frederick Ungar, 1960.

†Wedgwood, C. V., *The Thirty Years War.* Doubleday Anchor Books, 1961.

BIOGRAPHY

*Bainton, Roland H., *Here I Stand: A Life of Martin Luther.* Abingdon Press, 1951.

†Boehmer, Heinrich, *Martin Luther: Road to Reformation.* Transl. by John W. Doberstein and Theodore G. Tappert. Meridian Books, 1963.

Frame, Donald M., *Montaigne: A Biography.* Harcourt, Brace and World, 1965.

†Green, V.H.H., *Luther and the Reformation.* Capricorn Books, 1964.

†Huizinga, Johan, *Erasmus and the Age of Reformation.* Harper Torchbooks, 1957.

MacGregor, Geddes, *The Thundering Scot: A Portrait of John Knox.* The Westminster Press, 1957.

McNeill, John T., *The History and Character of Calvinism.* Oxford University Press, 1962.

*Neale, J. E., *The Age of Catherine de' Medici.* Barnes and Noble, 1959.

*Neale, J. E., *Queen Elizabeth I.* St. Martin's Press, 1959.

Schwiebert, E. G., *Luther and His Times.* Concordia Publishing House, 1950.

Wendel, François, *Calvin.* Transl. by Philip Mairet. Harper and Row, 1963.

THOUGHT AND CULTURE

*Artz, Frederick B., *From the Renaissance to Romanticism, Trends in Art, Literature, and Music, 1300-1830.* University of Chicago Press, 1962.

Boas, Marie, *The Scientific Renaissance 1450-1630.* Harper and Row, 1962.

*Cervantes, Miguel de, *Don Quixote.* 2 vols. Everyman's Library, 1954.

*Friedrich, Carl J., *The Age of the Baroque 1610-1660.* Harper and Row, 1952.

*Montaigne, Michel de, *Complete Essays of Montaigne.* Transl. by Donald M. Frame. Stanford University Press, 1958.

*More, Thomas, *Utopia.* Transl. by Turner. Penguin Books, 1966.

*Rabelais, François, *The Portable Rabelais.* Ed. and transl. by Samuel Putnam. Viking Press, 1946.

†Steinberg, S. H., *Five Hundred Years of Printing.* Penguin Books, 1962.

*Taylor, Henry Osborn, *Thought and Expression in the Sixteenth Century.* 2 vols. Frederick Ungar, 1959. (Paperback titles: *The Humanism of Italy, Erasmus and Luther, The French Mind, The English Mind, Philosophy and Science in the Sixteenth Century.*)

ART AND ARCHITECTURE

Descargues, Pierre, *Cranach.* Harry N. Abrams, 1962.

Gardner, Helen, *Art through the Ages.* 4th ed. Harcourt, Brace and World, 1959.

Gombrich, E. H., *The Story of Art.* 10th ed. Phaidon Publishers, 1962.

Huyghe, René, ed., *Larousse Encyclopedia of Renaissance and Baroque Art.* Prometheus Press, 1964.

Knappe, Karl-Adolf, *Albrecht Dürer, The Complete Engravings, Etchings, and Woodcuts.* Harry N. Abrams, 1965.

Panofsky, Erwin, *The Life and Art of Albrecht Dürer.* Princeton University Press, 1955.

Ruhmer, E., *Cranach.* Phaidon Publishers, 1963.

Simpson, Frederick M., *History of Architectural Development.* Vol. 4. *Renaissance Architecture* by J. Quentin Hughes and Norbert Lynton. David M. McKay, 1962.

Venturi, Lionello, *The Great Centuries of Painting, The Sixteenth Century.* Skira, World Publishing, 1956.

ECONOMICS

Clough, Shepard B., and Charles W. Cole, *Economic History of Europe.* 3rd ed. D. C. Heath, 1952.

Ehrenberg, Richard, *Capital and Finance in the Age of the Renaissance.* Transl. by H. M. Lucas. Augustus M. Kelley, 1963.

†Green, Robert W., ed., *Protestantism and Capitalism: The Weber Thesis and Its Critics.* D. C. Heath, 1959.

Samhaber, Ernst, *Merchants Make History.* Transl. by E. Osers. John Day, 1964.

Tawney, R. H., *The Agrarian Problem in the Sixteenth Century.* Burt Franklin, 1961.

ART INFORMATION AND PICTURE CREDITS

The sources for the illustrations in this book are set forth below. Credits for pictures that are positioned from left to right on a particular page are separated by semicolons; those positioned from top to bottom are separated by dashes. Photographers' names which follow a descriptive note are in parentheses. Abbreviations include "c." for century and "ca." for circa.

Cover—*Hands of an Apostle* by Albrecht Dürer, brush drawing, 1508, Graphische Sammlung Albertina, Vienna (Photo Meyer). 8-9—Map by David Greenspan.

CHAPTER 1: 10—Portrait of Martin Luther by Lucas Cranach the Elder, oil on wood, 1529, Uffizi Gallery, Florence (Skira). 13—A scholar and his pupils by Albrecht Dürer, woodcut, Germanisches Museum, Nuremberg (Friedrich Rauch). 14—Portrait of Hans Luther, Martin Luther's father, by Lucas Cranach the Elder, oil on wood, 1527, Wartburg Stiftung. 15—Portrait of Margarethe Luther, Martin Luther's mother, by Lucas Cranach the Elder, oil on wood, 1527, Wartburg Stiftung. 17—Map by David Greenspan. 19—*St. Peter's* by Marten van Heemskerck, drawing, ca. 1535, Furche Verlag, Hamburg. 21—Detail from *The Dance of the Peasants* by Pieter Brueghel the Elder, oil on wood, ca. 1568, Kunsthistorisches Museum, Vienna (Frank Lerner). 22-23—Detail from *The Dark Day* by Pieter Brueghel the Elder, oil on wood, 1565, Kunsthistorisches Museum, Vienna (Erich Lessing from Magnum); detail from *Dutch Kitchen* by Pieter Aertsen, oil on wood, ca. 1560, Museo Nazionale di S. Matteo, Pisa (David Lees). 24-25—*Spring* by Abel Grimer, oil on wood, ca. 1607, Musée des Beaux-Arts, Antwerp (Eddy Van Der Veen); *The Return of the Herd* by Pieter Brueghel the Elder, oil on wood, 1565, Kunsthistorisches Museum, Vienna (Erich Lessing from Magnum)—*Hay Harvest* by Pieter Brueghel the Elder, oil on wood, ca. 1565, National Gallery, Prague (Werner Forman); *Winter Scene* by Lucas van Valkenborch, oil on canvas, 1586, Kunsthistorisches Museum, Vienna (Erich Lessing from Magnum). 26—Detail from *The Peasant's Wedding* by Pieter Brueghel the Elder, oil on wood, ca. 1568, Kunsthistorisches Museum, Vienna (Frank Lerner). 27—Detail from *The Peasant's Wedding* by Pieter Brueghel the Elder, oil on wood, ca. 1568, Kunsthistorisches Museum, Vienna (Frank Lerner)—detail from *Wedding Dance* by Pieter Brueghel the Elder, oil on wood, 1566, Detroit Institute of Arts (Joseph Klima Jr.). 28-29—

The Carnival by Adriaen van de Venne, oil, mid-17th c., Chiaramonte-Bordonario Collection, Palermo (David Lees). 30-31—*Peasants Murdering a Soldier* by Marten van Clève, oil on wood, ca. 1566, Kunsthistorisches Museum, Vienna (Photo Meyer); *Massacre of the Innocents* by Pieter Brueghel the Elder, oil on wood, ca. 1563, Kunsthistorisches Museum, Vienna (Erich Lessing from Magnum). 32-33—*The Blind Leading the Blind* by Pieter Brueghel the Elder, tempera on canvas, 1568, Museo Nazionale di Capodimonte, Naples (David Lees).

CHAPTER 2: 34—View of Wartburg Castle, East Germany (Deutsche Fotothek, Dresden). 37—*Erasmus of Rotterdam* by Albrecht Dürer, engraving, 1526, Graphische Sammlung Albertina, Vienna. 40—Wittenberg Door (Bildarchiv Foto Marburg). 43—*Dr. Martin Luther in Pathmo, 1521* by Heinrich Göding, copper etching, 1598 (Photo Städtische Kulturinstitut Worms)—Papal Bull issued January 3, 1521 (Furche Verlag, Hamburg). 45—*Self-Portrait* as a 13-year-old boy by Albrecht Dürer, silverpoint drawing, 1484, Graphische Sammlung Albertina, Vienna. 46-47—*Knight, Death and the Devil* by Albrecht Dürer, engraving, 1513, Kupferstichkabinett, West Berlin; *Fool Addressing Geese and Swine* by Albrecht Dürer, woodcut from Sebastian Brant's *Das Narrenschyff* (Ship of Fools), 1494, Bayerische Staatsbibliothek, Munich (Friedrich Rauch); *Fool Putting Out His Neighbor's Fire Instead of His Own* by Albrecht Dürer, woodcut from Sebastian Brant's *Das Narrenschyff* (Ship of Fools), 1494, Bayerische Staatsbibliothek, Munich (Friedrich Rauch); *Fool in Ship* by Albrecht Dürer, woodcut from Sebastian Brant's *Das Narrenschyff* (Ship of Fools, 1494, Bayerische Staatsbibliothek, Munich (Friedrich Rauch); *Fool Addressing Geese and Swine* by Albrecht Dürer, woodcut from Sebastian Brant's *Das Narrenschyff* (Ship of Fools), 1494, Bayerische Staatsbibliothek, Munich (Friedrich Rauch). 48-49—*Apollo and Diana* by Albrecht Dürer, engraving, ca. 1505, Print Collection, The Metropolitan Museum of Art, New York, Fletcher Fund 1919 (Frank Lerner); *Battle of the Sea Gods* by Albrecht Dürer, pen and ink, 1494, Graphische Sammlung Albertina, Vienna. 50-51—*Flight into Egypt* from *The Life of Mary* by Albrecht Dürer, woodcut, ca. 1504, Staatliche Graphische Sammlung, Munich—*The Prodigal Son amid the Swine* by Albrecht Dürer, engraving, ca. 1496, Bibliothèque Nationale, Paris; *The Crucifixion* by Albrecht Dürer, woodcut, ca. 1497, from the *Large Passion* published 1511, Kupferstichkabinett, West Berlin (Robert Lackenbach from Black Star). 52—Detail from *The Four Horsemen* (Apocalypse), woodcut, ca. 1497, British Museum, London (John R. Freeman). 53—Detail from *St. Michael Fighting the Dragon* (Apocalypse), woodcut, ca. 1497, British Museum, London (John R. Freeman).

CHAPTER 3: 54—*Martin Luther and His Friends* by Lucas Cranach the Elder, oil, ca. 1530, Toledo Museum of Art, gift of Edward Drummond Libby (Jahn and Ollier Engraving Co.). 57—Portrait of *Akbar*, Great Mogul of India (1542-1605), pencil, 16th c., British Museum, London (The Bettmann Archive). 60—Portrait of John Calvin, oil, ca. 1564, Bibliothèque Publique et Universitaire de Genève, bequest of Henry Tronchin, 1925 (Yves Arnaud). 63—*Trial of Mary Queen of Scots*, pen-and-ink sketch of the arrangements for the trial at Fotheringhay Castle in 1586, preserved among papers of Robert Beale, Clerk of the Council of Elizabeth I, British Museum, London, Additional MS. 48027. 65—*The Money Lender and His Wife* by Quentin Massys, oil on wood, 1514, Louvre Museum, Paris (Claude Michaelides). 66-67—Double thaler of Frederick of Saxony, 1514—double thaler of Albert, Archbishop of Mainz, 1524—half thaler of Jacob Fugger, 1518—thaler of Charles V, 1543, American Numismatic Society, New York (Albert Fenn); detail from Miner's Altar by Hans Hesse in Church of St. Anne, Annaberg, Saxony, East Germany, oil on wood, 16th c. (Eric Schaal). 68-69—*Allegory of Trade* by Jost Amman, woodcut, 1585, Germanisches Nationalmuseum, Nuremberg (Keyssersche Verlagsbuchhandlung, Munich). 70—*The Card Players* by Lucas van Leyden, oil on wood, early 16th c., National Gallery of Art, Washington, D.C., Samuel H. Kress Collection—sale of indulgences by Jorg Breu, woodcut, ca. 1530 (The Bettmann Archive). 71—*The Payment* by Lucas Cranach the Elder, oil on wood, 1532, National Museum, Stockholm (Hans Hammarskjold of Tio Photographers). 72-73—*Schuldbrief* to Anton Fugger the Younger from Graf von Rechberg, 1539, Fugger Museum, Babenhausen, Swabia (Eric Schaal)—Jacob Fugger's correspondence chest, Fugger Museum, Babenhausen, Swabia (Eric Schaal); *Jacob Fugger with His Secretary* (Bookkeeper) by Matthäus Schwartz, aquarelle on paper, 1516, Herzog Anton Ulrich Museum, Braunschweig (Eric Schaal). 74-75—Antwerp Stock Exchange, engraving, mid-16th c. (Radio Times Hulton Picture Library, London).

CHAPTER 4: 76—*Lyon's Church Named Paradise* by Jean Perrissin, 16th c., Bibliothèque Publique et Universitaire de Genève (Yves Debraine). 79—*Handstone of Francis I Kneeling before Charles V* by Caspar Ulrich, after 1550, Kunsthistorisches Museum, Vienna. 82-83—Portrait of Henry VIII by unknown artist, oil, late 16th c., National Portrait Gallery, London; portrait of Edward VI as Prince of Wales by Hans Holbein the Younger, oil and tempera on wood, 1543, The Metropolitan Museum of Art, New York, Bache Collection (The Bettmann Archive); portrait of Mary Tudor by Master John, oil, 1544, National Portrait Gallery, London; portrait of Charles V (Culver Pictures); portrait of William of Orange by Adriaen Thomasz, oil, 1578, Photo Commissie, Rijksmuseum, Amsterdam. 89—*Elizabeth and Fame*, woodcut from *A Book Containing Divers Sorts of Hands* by Sir William Teshe, 1589, by courtesy of the Trustees of the British Museum, London. 90-91—*Birds-eye Plan of London*, engraving by Franz Hogenberg from *Civitates orbis terrarum* by Braun, 1574, Cologne, courtesy Folger Shakespeare Library, Washington, D.C. (Henry Beville). 92-93—Illustrations from *Album of Tobias Delhafen of Nuremburg* and *Album of George Holzschuher of Nuremburg*, early 17th Century, by courtesy of the Trustees of the British Museum, London. 94-95—*The Queen Opening a New Parliament in the White Chamber*, engraving from *Nobilitas politica vel civilis* by Robert Glover, 1608, courtesy Folger Shakespeare Library, Washington, D.C. (Henry Beville)—*Eastcheap Market* and *Billingsgate*, drawings from *A Caveat of the City of London* by Hugh Alley, 1598, courtesy Folger Shakespeare Library, Washington, D.C. (Henry Beville). 96-97—*The Palace of Nonsuch with a Royal Progress of Queen Elizabeth*, drawing by George Hoefnagel, 1568, courtesy of the Trustees of the British Museum, London (John R. Freeman). 98-99—Illustrations from *Stam Boek of Michael Van Meer*, early 17th Century, courtesy Edinburgh University, Scotland.

CHAPTER 5: 100—*Celebration of the Centenary of the Jesuit Order* by Andrea Sacchi and Jan Miel, oil, 1639, Galleria Nazionale Palazzo Barberini, Rome (Emmett Bright). 102—Page from Polyglot Bible from Alcala de Herares, Spain, 1514-1517, Rare Book Division, New York Public Library (Frank Lerner). 106—Map of Jesuit edifices in Rome, 17th c., Gabinetto Nazionale delle Stampe, Rome (Oscar Savio). 109—Council of Trent by unknown artist, detached fresco, 17th c., Secretariat of State, Vatican (David Lees). 110-111—Fresco by Il Domenichino, Cathedral of Naples, Chapel of Saint Januarius, early 17th c., (Aldo Durazzi); *The Trinity* or *Christ in the Arms of the Eternal Father* by El Greco, oil on canvas, ca. 1577, Prado, Madrid (Fernand Bourges). 112-113—*Charles Borromeo among Plague Victims* by Orazio Borgianni, oil on canvas, ca. 1610, Casa Generalizia Padri Mercedari, Rome (David Lees); *Saint Martin and the Beggar* by El Greco, oil on canvas, 1604-1614, National Gallery of Art, Washington, D.C., Andrew Mellon Collection. 114—*Jesuits at the Court of Akbar*, manuscript illumination by Nar-Singh, ca. 1605, from Akbar Nama Folio 263 verso, Chester Beatty Collection, Dublin (Rex Roberts Studios, Dublin). 115—*Priest and Two Children* by Nobukata, color on paper, late 16th c., Kobe Municipal Museum (T. Tanuma)—detail from *Southern Barbarian Screen* by Kanō Naizen, color on gold paper, early 17th c., Kobe Municipal Art Gallery and the *Horizon History of Christianity*. 116-117—*Saint Bartholomew's Day Massacre* by François Dubois, oil, 16th c., Musée Cantonal des Beaux-Arts, Lausanne (Yves Debraine). 118-119—Details from *Expeditionis Hispanorum in Angliam, vera descripto*, charts by Robert Adams engraved by Augustine Ryther, hand-colored engravings, 1590, courtesy British Museum, London; *Spanish Armada*, wood diptych in St. Faith's Church, Gaywood, Kings Lynn, Norfolk, late 16th c. (Derek Bayes). 120-121—*The Battle of Rocroi* by Sauveur Le Conte, oil on canvas, 1643, Musée Condé, Chantilly (Derek Bayes).

CHAPTER 6: 122—Frontispiece from Martin Luther's translation of the Bible, woodcut, 1534, Rare Book Division, New York Public Library (Frank Lerner). 124—Chart by Matt Greene. 127—Montaigne's tower at Saint Michel de Montaigne near Bordeaux (Dr. Merly). 129—Map from Thomas More's *Utopia* by Ambrosius Holbein, 1518, Historisches Bildarchiv, Bad Berneck. 130—Detail of London scene by Claes Jansz Visscher, engraving, 1616, Map Division, New York Public Library—interior of Swan Theater, London, by Arends van Buchell, pen and ink, ca. 1596, University of Utrecht. 133—A printing shop by Theodor Galle, copperplate from Jan van der Straet's *Nova Reperta*, 1638 (The Bettmann Archive). 134—A form cutter, from Jost Amman's *Staendebuch*, woodcut, 1568, Deutsches Museum, Munich—a scribe by Albrecht von Eybe, illustration from *Spiegel der Sitten*, woodcut, 1511, Historisches Bildarchiv, Bad Berneck; illuminated letter from Justemont Abbey Bible, French, 1170-1180, pen on vellum, Private Collection (Dr. H. Zinram). 135—Page from Biblia Pauperum, woodcut from block book Bible, Netherlands, 1470, British Museum, London (Derek Bayes). 136-137—A type caster, from Jost Amman's *Staendebuch*, woodcut, 1568, Deutsches Museum, Munich; diagram by Matt Greene—construction of letter "Q" by geometrical principles from Sigismundo de Fanti's *Theorica et Pratica*, 1514 (Frank Lerner). 138-139—A printing shop by Jost Amman, woodcut, 16th c., Historisches Bildarchiv, Bad Berneck—diagram by Matt Greene. 140—Page from First Book of Chronicles, facsimile edition of Gutenberg Bible of 1455, Rare Book Division, New York Public Library (Frank Lerner). 141—Page from *Nuremberg Chronicles* by Hartmann Schedel, printed by Anton Koberger, 1493, Rare Book Division, New York Public Library (Frank Lerner); title page from *A Sermon on the New Testament: That is, the Holy Mass* by Martin Luther, printed in Wittenberg, 1520, Bibliothèque Publique et Universitaire de Genève—page from *Poliphili Hypnerotomachia* by Francesco Colonna, printed by Aldous Manutius, 1499, Rare Book Division, New York Public Library (Frank Lerner); title page from *De Bonis Operibus* by Martin Luther, printed by Johannus Grunenberg, 1521, Rare Book Division, New York Public Library (Frank Lerner).

CHAPTER 7: 142—Geometric landscapes from *Geometria et Perspectiva* by Lorenz Stoer, woodcuts, 1567, New York Public Library. 145—Anatomical studies by Andreas Vesalius, woodcuts, 1543, from *Icones anatomicae*, New York: New York Academy of Medicine, 1934, courtesy of the New York Academy of Medicine Library. 146—Portrait of Anna Meyer by Hans Holbein the Younger, pastel, ca. 1520, Kunstmuseum Basel, Kupferstichkabinett, from *Great Drawings of All Time*, Volume II, Shorewood Publishers, 1962. 149—Decorative letter by Johann Theodor de Bry, engraving, 1595, Staatliche Graphische Sammlung, Munich, from *Gebrauchsgraphik*, May 1965. 151—Staircase of the château at Blois, Loire-et-Cher, France, built 1515 to 1524 (J. R. Johnson from Rapho Guillumette). 152-153—Monastery of Certosa di Pavia near Milan, built 1396-1507 (Marzari); pen-and-ink drawings by Zena Bernstein. 154-155—Pen-and-ink drawings by Zena Bernstein—château at Chambord, Loire-et-Cher, France, built 1537-1550 (J. R. Johnson from Rapho Guillumette). 156-157—Pen-and-ink drawings by Zena Bernstein; castle wing at Heidelberg, Germany, built 1556 to 1559 (Mark Kauffman). 158—Tour d'Aigues, Vaucluse Department, Southern France, built 1571 (Mark Kauffman). 159—Town Hall of Antwerp, Belgium, built 1561-1565 (Mark Kauffman); façade of Burghley House in Northants, England, built 1585, photograph courtesy the Marquess of Exeter (Brian Seed). 160-161—Petit château at Chantilly, Oise Department, Northern France, built ca. 1560 (Pierre Boulat).

CHAPTER 8: 163—Detail from Miner's Altar by Hans Hesse in Church of St. Anne, Annaberg, Saxony, East Germany, oil on wood, 16th c. (Eric Schaal). 164—The Copernican Universe, illustration from *A Prognostication Everlasting . . . Containing Rules to Judge the Weather* by Leonard Digges, 1576, The Granger Collection, New York. 169—Duke Christian of Brunswick and cities made famous by his name, copper etching, ca. 1622, Landesmuseum für Kunst und Kulturgeschichte, Münster (Greve and Brummel, Münster). 171-181—Photographs by John Launois from Black Star.

ACKNOWLEDGMENTS

The editors are indebted to Claus-Peter Clasen, Assistant Professor of History, Yale University; Colin Eisler, Associate Professor, Institute of Fine Arts, New York University; Bates Lowry, Professor of Art, Brown University; Rev. Eugene V. Clark, Cardinal Spellman High School, New York; Rev. Wilhelm Pauck, Professor of Church History, Union Theological Seminary; Henry Grunthal, Curator, American Numismatics Society; J. Ben Lieberman, Communication Consultant, Popular Printing Company, New York; David Zubin, Columbia University; Louis B. Wright, Director, The Folger Shakespeare Library, Washington, D.C.; Oskar Thulin, Lutherhalle, Wittenberg; Erich Steingräber, General Director, and Fritz Zink, Germanisches National Museum, Nuremberg; Ernst Holzinger, Städelsches Kunstinstitut, Frankfurt; Jan Lautz, Staatliche Kunstalhalle, Karlsruhe; Helmut Presser, Gutenberg Museum, Mainz; Haldor Söhner, Alte Pinakothek, Munich; Klaus Popitz, Staatliche Museen Zu Berlin, Kupferstichkabinett; Georg Illert, Kulturinstitut, Worms; Gräfin Preysing, Baron Gotz von Pöllnitz, Fürstliche Gräfliche Fuggersche Stiftungs-Administration; Wartburg Foundation, Eisenach; Melanchton Verein, Bretten; Gustav Hofmann, General Director, Bayerische Staatsbibliothek; Heinz Zirnbauer, Stadtbibliothek, Nuremberg; Hans-Heinrich Richter, Deutsche Fotothek, Dresden; Lolo Handke, Historisches Bildarchiv, Bad Berneck; Charlotte Fremke, Historia Foto, Bad Sachsa; Wilfried Göpel, Archiv für Kunst und Geschichte, Berlin; Bildarchiv Foto, Marburg; Furche Verlag, Hamburg; Erwin M. Auer, Director, Georg Kugler, Dozent Hans Wagner, Kunsthistorisches Museum, Vienna; Haus-Hof und Staatsarchiv, Vienna; National Portrait Gallery, London; Science Museum, London; Department of Prints and Drawings, British Museum, London; Italo Faldi, Director, Galleria Nazionale Barberini, Rome; Roma Mezzetti, Gabinetto Nazionale delle Stampe, Rome; Isv Umberto Damiani Chiesa del Gesù, Rome; Vatican Library, Rome; Curia Generalizia dell'Ordine delle Mercede, Curia Generalizia della Compagnia di Gesù, Rome; Soprintendenza al Monumenti, Milan; Raffaelle Causa, Director, Galleria Nazionale di Capodimonte, Naples; Baroness Beatrice Chiaramonte-Bordonario Collection, Palermo; Museo Civico, Pisa; Pasteur Henri Bosc, Société de L'Histoire du Protestantisme Français.

INDEX

PRINTED IN U.S.A.